****

Copyright © 2022 by Eliza Jong
All rights reserved. This book or any portion thereof may not be reproduced or used in any manner whatsoever without the express written permission of the publisher except for the use of brief quotations in a book review.
Printed in the United Kingdom
First Printing, 2022
ISBN 9798842303113
Independently published

About the Author

Eliza Jong is a Yorkshire lass born and bred. She lives there with her husband, 2 beautiful if not slightly feral children, 2 crazy dogs, a lizard and until recently some goldfish which have thankfully now all died. Big on honesty and not great at sugar coating anything, she likes to write about her family and everyday life as a mum, wife, avid supporter of women and her love for anything rude, lewd and inappropriate. She works at a bank part time but her true calling is being a mum and homemaker. Her hobbies include fantasising about cake, reading crime thrillers whilst eating cake and sneaking around during the night to secretly eat more cake.

You can visit Eliza on Instagram at @life_by_eliza or check out her website at http://www.lifebyeliza.com where you can read her blogs.

If you're feeling brave there's also Life by Eliza the Podcast available on Google Podcasts, Apple Podcasts, Spotify and Anchor FM

I've only been Kidnapped Twice

Eliza Jong

****

Contents

Note to Reader - An Introduction

Point of Reference; People who might appear in my stories

A Natural born cleaner, or not

I am an excellent Driver

Andy Suck on these

I now pronounce you Husband and Shit Machine

I've only been Kidnapped Twice

A Bat out of Hell will be gone when the Morning comes (hopefully)

The Worst Cafe Ever

Next to Rule the World is a French Icon

Pirate Dreams

The House that Husband Built, not Jack

An Accomplice to Murder

The Drug Dealers Villa

Shiatsu Practitioner or Professional Sexual Preditor

Country Living

And then there were three

15 Fun Facts about Pregnancy, Birth and the Aftermath

Note to reader - An Introduction

Everything you are about to read in this book is true. By true I mean categorically and completely 100% true. Not, there are elements of truth in it, or that these accounts are based on true stories.

They are totally true.

These experiences and observations make up my life and have been partly responsible for shaping me into the odd, fairly tolerant, except when I'm not, some would say crazy Human I am today. They are life lessons. All sent specifically to me to learn from, as your own experiences are sent especially for you, whether you choose to acknowledge this or not. Whether it's being kidnapped, misplacing our 3 year old in Spain or my views and observations about housekeeping (or something with an invariable amount of humdrum), all are equally as important and I have written about both the unforgettable and the everyday mundane stuff. I saw a quote on Pinterest once that said, 'My life is one long humiliation separated by snacks,' and I could really relate to that. I learnt a long time ago that when things happen that are sometimes out of the ordinary, or completely ordinary but with lashings of embarrassment thrown in, you should welcome them with open arms, like you chose it. Whatever is mapped out for us will happen anyway. You can dig your nails in and cling tightly to your dignity, kicking, screaming, resisting whilst chorusing, 'Why me?,' or you can buckle up, throw your arms in the air, feel the wind on your face and enjoy the thrill of the ride, a large proportion of the time through gritted teeth understandably. If it's something really terrible or particularly degrading, take comfort in the fact that you can always tell someone a story about it later to make them smile and see their horror, and all the while helping you get over your ordeal through the power of sharing.

Occasionally in the book there might be the odd account here and there not actually about me, but told from my perspective. If my life lesson wasn't to shit myself at my own wedding then I can guarantee I know someone who's was.

So, just to recap, all accounts and stories in this book are not 'based on', 'loosely related to' or 'have elements of' the truth. They are wholly and fully, without omission, kick me in the crutch sincerely truthful. A small snippet into the blessing / debacle that is my life.

I have included a few short descriptions of the people who may appear in these accounts, who are mainly family, friends and dogs. This is for point of reference. It's a pet peeve of mine when you can't fully enjoy the story because you're trying to work out who people are and what they're about. So I've literally done all the work. There's nothing else to do except kick back with a brew and enjoy.

Happy reading.

Point of Reference; People who might feature in my stories

I thought this little run down of people who feature in my stories might give some background to the sort of characters they are. You might be wondering why I never mention names? This is purely to spare anyone any unwanted embarrassment, and to give the gift of deniability that they were ever involved at all in anything you read in this book, but rest assured they absolutely were, and are all very real people.

Husband
The man who is exactly that. My Husband. Together for 19 years, we have been married for 12. One of his favourite things is to pretend that he was forced to marry me, completely against his will. A true romantic. He is one of life's truth tellers. He nearly always has an opinion, even when you wish he wouldn't. And never minces his words, even when you wish he would. A father to our children, the

Anklebiters, he also has two grown up daughters who have proved to be bright young women that are both a force to be reckoned with. Although not a natural face stroker, or one for romantic mumbo jumbo, he is loyal, hard working and generous. He is unequivocally stubborn and can at times appear to be long suffering, which undoubtedly is absolutely deliberate. He loves motorbikes. Mostly fast expensive ones that he would go any length to own, even if it means having to sell a child to finance it. **It's ok he'll have three left**. He fancies himself as a survivalist and often dreams about us living off grid, in a pit or cave with no amenities, for fun. In some ways not a modern man and on occasion his views could leave anyone wondering if he'd come straight out of the stone age. His wit is dry and occasionally his temper can be short which deems him unintentionally funny, making me laugh when I should be defending my side of the argument, women's rights or something else that is equally as important.

The Anklebiters

Our beloved, if not slightly feral children. Currently 14 and 11 years old. A gorgeous girl and a beautiful boy.

Grown up Girls
Husband's older girls, both in their late twenties. To which I am a proud step mum and a merciless instigator of making them call me mummy, especially when I am a bit drunk. One of their favourite things is when I completely show myself up. They wildly encourage this, and sometimes film it.

Mother In Law
Husband's mother. One of the funniest ladies I've ever met. Never short of a story, she is well known in her local area for her friendly, helpful disposition. She is a doting Grandma and in days gone by, not one to shy away from dragging a tarpaulin of builders' sand into her living room so the children can play in the 'sand pit' on a rainy day. She will do anything for anyone, which usually involves pimping out Father In Law to do jobs, give lifts, and single-handedly collect and deliver shopping to the whole street or similar.

Father In Law
Mother In Laws bitch. I'm joking. Husband's dad. Married to Mother In Law since God was a boy. Dedicated Grandad, local football team supporter, and beer drinker. He is the number one lift giver of the family and can be relied upon to rescue us from almost any location worldwide at any time during the day or night. A keen gardener, he is also the owner of the most beautiful hanging baskets in Yorkshire.

Dad
My Dad. Mum's first husband of 20 years. An Engineer by trade, he is a genius in the building or fixing of any known object in the world, **except my Karcher steam cleaner it would seem - I'm not sure you put your back into that one Dad.** A motor enthusiast, he boasts an exceptional amount of knowledge of anything car-related and is also partial to a motorbike. A dedicated musician, he plays guitar and still attends lessons after many years, because everyday is a school day. He likes to make us listen to his new musical

arrangements, much to the Anklebiters dismay and to my joy because I like to sing along, much to Dad's dismay. He is Wednesday afternoon school picker upper and, according to the youngest Anklebiter, makes the best chicken sandwiches in the universe.

Mum
My mum. Very glamorous and 'with it'. Lover of children so long as they are her own grandchildren, with no exceptions to this rule. Chief babysitter. Dislikes crowds and random people and loves home and family. She has a shoe collection that would rival Emelda Marcos' and is a sewing extraordinaire who can cleverly throw together curtains, clothes and face masks with ease, and does so frequently at my request.

Step Dad
Mum's Husband and general partner in crime. A professional DIYer and committed cyclist, he could win an award for tidiness. If you foolishly turn your back on your cup of coffee for longer than a nanosecond, he will swipe it and wash it up immediately, whether you have finished or

not. He is also fun grandad. The grandad that is not against a bit of rough and tumble and has the Anklebiters going wild and behaving even more feral than usual. He has also been known to use a child's fishing net in the art of bat capture.

Auntie
My Auntie, my mum's sister and the Anklebiters Great Auntie. In charge of the school run on a Monday. She is the eldest Anklebiters' best friend and Nintendo Switch animal crossing trainee, as instigated by her best friend. She is the best house cleaner and the most organised person I know. A keen golfer. She is also the owner of hanging baskets that could rival Father In Laws.

Brother
One of my 2 brothers. Three years younger than me, we are similar in looks and could be mistaken for each other when he wears a dress (more frequently than you might think). *Stag do's and fancy dress. What were you thinking?* Or when I've neglected facial

waxing and my beard is thriving. Partial to a belly laugh, he is jolly, thoughtful and kind.

A little update about the story that features my brother. It's not actually in the book. I replaced it with another one at the last minute but have decided to keep this description of him so he doesn't cry about it.

The Bride
My friend who I've known for 20 years. We are both low maintenance and expect very little from each other. We have a mutual understanding that birthdays, Christmas and regular telephone calls hold no place in our relationship. Always there for each other, it goes without saying that each would be instantly available for the other when needed. When I say 'when needed' this could be anything from 'needing' a good night out to blow off some steam or 'needing' a kidney. She is always supportive, rarely gets cross and never judges. Even when I leave tit prints on her patio door after a particularly good party.

The Hairdressers

2 of my crazier friends. Once owned a hair salon together which always felt more like a comedy club than a hairdressers. Stalkers of celebrities, lovers of a good night out and very close friends with Jack Daniels. One of them once made up and performed a rap, off the cuff at an interview for a position at an exclusive hair salon **which she got, obviously.** Life and soul of most parties.

The Work Girls
A group of ladies, *I use this term loosely,* that I have had the pleasure of working with for a long time. Some as many as 15 years. We work together in the bank and know each other well. A little too well due to more than occasional over-sharing. There seems to be no filter or secrets in our workplace, making it 'the norm' to know everything about each other, even down to anal warts. Always up for having a laugh and always there for each other, they are much more than my work colleagues but also dear friends **and certainly not ladies as I indicated earlier.**

The Gentle Giant

Husband's friend. Loyal, kind and always there to help in any way he can. He is very funny and has a mean set of storytelling skills which we all relish on each visit. When he drops by it's never with notice and always at a ridiculously early hour usually over a weekend. He has a huge personality and has tendencies to rescue residents from the animal kingdom should they need it. Mostly dogs but there was a time he drove around for a week with a van load of badly done to chinchillas attempting to rehome every single one. He is also the most frightening looking man you'll ever lay eyes on. Covered in tattoos, the sort that scream of a prison stay and nod to a colourful life, he has a huge stance, a beard and an extremely loud voice.

The Dogs
Our old handsome Bully. 13 years old. Mostly smells of feet and is usually in need of a breath mint. Lover of shoes, cake, midget gems, sunbathing and sleeping. He is now a companion to our new dog, a little beast of a French Bulldog who constantly wees and poos anywhere in the house that is carpeted and

especially off limits. She is 3 years old and only has two known facial expressions.
 1. Surprised.
 2. Pissed off.

A Natural Born Cleaner, or not

I am filthy.

And I don't mean in the way most men dream of.

This is what I mean …

- No one can tell if a bowl, cup or spoon has been washed or just been left to dry and put back in the cupboard.

Until recently we have always had a dishwasher, until the useless thing gave up the ghost, forcing me to get involved with washing up. My technique needs work but who wants to practice pot washing?

- Using a pair of dirty knickers off the bedroom floor to dust, in the absence of an actual duster being instantly to hand.

There are not enough hours in the day to run up and down two or three flights of stairs to the cleaning drawer for a duster everytime I stumble on a dust bomb

situation when there's a perfectly good pair of knickers available.

- Realising that the dust on the top of the door frames is so thick, you might need to get the jet wash out.

I am 5ft 6, My eyeline is far lower than the top of the door frames. I only remember to look up once every 5 years.

- Attempting to clean my copper pans and thinking I have ruined them by turning them a pale pink colour. On further investigation I realise that is the colour they are meant to be. Not black with dark brown edging.

Similar care procedure to a wok. Do not wash after use, just rinse, wipe and don't look too closely or whilst wearing glasses.

- In spring when our small white dog is moulting, the whole downstairs looks like we've had a new luxurious thick white carpet fitted … until autumn.

Who wants to spend 23 out of 24 hours a day vacuuming only for the little beast to move just once during the hour I'm not vacuuming and re carpet the whole kitchen.

- Carpet Moths

I can't discuss this matter any further. It's too traumatic. It makes me have tit sweats. For those who are interested, this story can be found on my blog.

- The oven. A disaster zone.

Current oven : 18 months without a clean and counting.

I could go on . . . And on . . . and on . . .

The oven. Oh shit a brick, the oven. I am an avid cook and use my oven constantly. When I've finished preparing and cooking a meal or baking a batch of buns **(just call me Fanny Craddick)** I don't want to then set about performing a deep clean on it. Or even wiping it. I promise myself that I'll do that before I use it the next time. But I never do. Consequently it's rare that I can see through the glass doors, and who knew that the shelves were once a silver colour and not black? A bizarre revelation. 'Gross,' I hear you baulk, and you are correct. I am pretty gross.

Before we moved out of our last house I contemplated what I would do about the oven. It was a beautiful stainless steel range cooker. Two ovens and a six ring gas hob. But having limped through 4 years without a clean was not looking or smelling it's best. After considering the options

1. Clean it myself

2. Hire a professional oven cleaner and face the embarrassment of my own filth

I decided on the latter. Having given all the particulars of the oven to the lady over the phone she assured me it would be no problem. It would take approximately 3-4 hours and look like a new pin on completion. All for the bargain price of £120. **Christ on a bike.** I had to arrange it for when Husband would be at work and then shamelessly pass it off as my own efforts. Not adverse to spending money in any way, I know that the knowledge of paying someone to come and clean our oven, something that should fall under my housewife duties would make him heave.

That poor lady. She arrived at 8am and got to work. I don't embarrass easily, but when she was still working hard at 3pm, the oven in pieces all over the kitchen floor, it was slightly awkward. She eventually finished at just before 5pm. That's close to 9 hours to clean my oven. She certainly earned her money that day.

I have no problem accepting that I am a blameless victim of simply being a rubbish cleaner. I try hard, I put the effort in but when the jobs are done and it's time to admire the handy work I've spent all day perfecting, quite honestly it looks no different. It's enough to make anyone throw themselves under a bus. On the odd occasion when I have worked especially hard and I can detect a minuscule difference my heart is full, my life complete. The house proud demon is unleashed. Everything is slightly cleaner, a little tidier, less smudgy, but I can not congratulate myself and celebrate because two days later I have to do it all over again. And so it goes on. The hamster wheel of housework never ends. EVER.

In my experience everyone has that particular friend that adores cleaning. A Monica Gellar type. As the day breaks they're up and out of bed like they've shit it. Eagerly getting into their joggers and wriggling into their marigolds, excitement building as they collect their special cleaning kit from the utility room. Every imaginable spray, polish and sponge they could need for every imaginable job.

It's what they live for.

I have a couple of friends that are this way. If I'm honest I'm a bit jealous.

Imagine doing something you love that is mutually beneficial to everyone living in your home.

Imagine not being scared that when you have your Monica friend over for coffee she'll pull out a pair of white inspection gloves.

Imagine actually welcoming a white glove inspection because you know your home is spotless.

Imagine not congratulating yourself when you've had company over and they leave without catching dysentery.

Imagine not entering the living room you keep 'for best' and finding a dog poo.

Just imagine.

Can we include clothes washing within the housework bracket? I am going to include it because I actually excel at it. I am an excellent washer. There's nothing like it when you remove a clean load and hang it out to dry on the line on a good drying day. **What am I? A seventy year old woman?** The smell of lenor drifting over your garden. I genuinely love it. It's because of this great passion for doing the laundry *(I realise I'm not American but what's the English equivalent?)* that if the washing basket is empty I resort to washing the lone dirty tea towel or random jacket lurking on the hook that no one has worn since last winter. I can't get enough.

Everyone loves an invitation to have coffee at a friend's house, so when I received one from one of my Monica Gellar type friends it was very welcome. She wasn't a close friend, more of an acquaintance but a jolly was a jolly so I went along. Anything to avoid a morning of cleaning.

I stopped on the way for cream cakes. You can always count on me to bring cake. Walking up the front garden path towards the pristine, recently washed front door, I observed how remarkably see through the living room windows looked. I realise all windows are see through, it's just some of them, like mine, are more difficult to see through than others. After being invited in I was led into the kitchen. The large shiny kitchen was near empty, completely free of clutter and looked like it had been cleaned to within an inch of its life by a crime scene clean up crew. It was comparable to a show kitchen you might see in B&Q or on Pinterest. I'd settled against the breakfast bar side of the work top. Still standing up we chatted for a while until the coffee was brewed and the cakes had been put on a special cake plate, on a tray, with a flower. *I'm not even kidding.* Sweeping into the living room, tray in hand , she rested it down on the highly polished glass coffee table next to the extensive selection of glossy magazines. Excusing herself she said she wouldn't be a minute. Looking around the living room, the level of neatness and order was outstanding. It was truly immaculate. I wiggled my bare toes into the carpet. It had a thick pile and had been vacuumed into lines. The pale grey settee was smooth and clean, and there wasn't a dog hair in sight. I wanted to sit down but couldn't see anywhere suitable. There were two different kinds of cushions on each of the two seater sofas, standing to attention. A mixture of soft pink mohair and grey sequins. I was still trying to decide the best place to sit, where I would make the least amount of disruption when she returned. 'Excuse the mess,' she giggled, 'it's cleaning day today.'

Unbelievable.

I am an excellent Driver

My first car was a white Vauxhall Nova. My first 3 cars were actually all white Vauxhall Novas. Not because I'm strangely obsessed with them but Dad was in charge of anything to do with cars in our household at the time and there was no way I was getting a shiny new expensive one on finance like my friends when I could have a rickety old Nova, without power steering and with an old fashioned choke before the days of fuel injection. And to get me 3 on the trot, he also clearly thought that Nova's ruled. If you are under the age of 30 there's a strong possibility you have no idea what a Nova looks like. If you are a child of the 80's there is an equally strong possibility that a Nova was also your first car. All my Nova's had names because why wouldn't they? You get a cat, you name it. You have a baby, you name it. You have an array of plants in your kitchen, you name them. It's a ridiculous notion to have a car and not name it. My first one was called Seth.

Nova Number 1- Seth

I awoke on my 18th birthday to find him parked on the driveway wearing a big red ribbon. After borrowing my grandad's Corsa now and again for the previous 6 months since passing my driving test, the concept of having a car of my very own, to use as and when I wanted was the most exciting thing that had ever happened to me. Coming and going as I pleased without having to rely on anyone was my introduction to complete independence. Hand selected by Dad, an expert in anything car related I knew Seth would be safe, economical to run, cheap to insure and I absolutely loved him. I couldn't wait to take Dad out in my very own car to show off my driving skills and make him proud of his little girl. In reality he spent most of the journey tensely clutching the underside of the passenger seat with both hands and gasping loudly each time I approached a roundabout or junction. He kept a close eye on how fast we were going, which was not within the speed limit because back then I was even worse for speeding then I am now, and I'm still pretty bad now, but it was ok, I knew he secretly liked it. I have found over the years that when Dad pretends to disapprove of certain things it's a blatant cover for his hidden amusement, which

I love and even now as a grown woman only encourages me. On returning to the safety of our driveway Dad escaped and Mum became my next victim. We drove to McDonalds for my birthday breakfast, just us girls and I have to say that it's still one of my nicest memories. There was no gasping or clutching either, she had faith in my driving which was probably fairly similar to her own style and only confirmed that there really wasn't anything to be concerned over and that Dad was just being a drama queen.

My second Nova was called Ray because he was a sporty Nova Sting, and that made him a 'Stingray'. Very cool, I know. My third and final Nova was called Bob. He would be my last car of the Nova persuasion and would last me until I was introduced to Hector, a black Citroen Saxo that I thought was the dog's bollocks after years of enduring Nova's. Hector even had power steering and electric windows. I'd finally made it. What I haven't mentioned was that the reason each of my cars replaced each other was that I may have, possibly, now and again, had my fair share of accidents in them, always resulting in them becoming a right off and dying in the end.

Seth (first car) met his fate when a bus crashed into him. Well not actually into him but into the car behind him, causing a dramatic pile up that involved 4 cars and a bus, with me and Seth sandwiched right in the middle. Each car was squashed into the next because the bus driver was nosy parkering at something more interesting than the road so he never saw the vehicle in front. Luckily I hung on to my life unlike poor Seth, and in addition I came away with a small whiplash claim. It was shortly after this that dad found Ray for me. Ray (second car) became part of the family and served me well, collecting a few parking tickets along the way as Seth had, but essentially filling the job of loyal servant until there was an incident with an ambulance. After pulling into the side of the road to let it pass like any sensible road user, the car behind tried to overtake and follow the ambulance resulting in it crashing into me (or me crashing into it) when I pulled back out into the road. That wasn't the one that finished him off though. It was a sad day when I reversed out of the driveway onto the main road we lived on when the approaching car veered onto my side of the road and crashed into me. **It's gradually** *dawning on me that there appears to be a running theme here. Why do people always crash into me? It cannot possibly be in any way ,shape or form my fault because just for the record, I am an excellent driver.*

Following an exchange of insurance particulars I called my insurance company to fill them in on all the details, this is when it became clear the knobrash that was driving the other car wasn't insured and had fed me a pack of lies and given me a shit load of false details. We waved goodbye to Ray, making way for Bob who would be the last of the Nova's. Bob (third car) was also involved in the art of parking ticket collection, the occasional speeding fine and had the worst personal hygiene of any car in existence. Regularly concealing uneaten food, old McDonalds wrappers and oddly, a BBQ bottle that lived on the passenger seat for approximately 6 months one summer, but more importantly he was also the culprit that reversed over Husbands beloved sports car.

Let me explain.

It was the summer that Husband and I met, and this fateful day also happened to be my 23rd birthday. Although our relationship was new, things had progressed quickly and I had moved in. If this ever comes up in conversation Husband tells people that dont know better than to resist his lies, that I moved in without his permission and he has been trying to get rid of me ever since. Nice. Also highly untrue. Anyway… It was my birthday, Husband had booked us a table somewhere fancy to eat that evening, I was in good spirits having received a torrent of Happy Birthday messages and was about to go and get in Bob and make my way to work. Life was good. The parking situation at our old house was less than ideal and it was always survival of the fittest between the neighbours to see who could get one of the limited parking spaces down the tenfoot. **Tenfoot - a term used in the Yorkshire region to describe the 10 foot wide alley that runs at the back of a row of terraced houses.** I usually did my best to get right on the end next to the fence so I could easily back out without getting hemmed in by over enthusiastic parkers who didn't leave enough room for me to manoeuvre. In fact it was rare that I parked anywhere else and I came to know it as my spot. So full of the joys of my life, and lost in my own thoughts of birthday treats, birthday meals, and generally wrapped up in my own world, I didn't notice that Bob was not in his usual spot. I must have parked further forward than usual because Husband had managed to park his Mitsubishi FTO, his pride and joy directly behind me, only I hadn't noticed. Trapped in my own bubble of birthday smugness I had been away with the fairies when I had climbed into Bob, put him in reverse and slammed my foot down, reversing straight over Husband's sports car. I say 'reversed over' his car instead of 'into' his car because the bonnet on his car was so stupidly low that not only did I smash into it but Bob actually mounted the bonnet and backed over it slightly. His prized possession. It was one of those times when I really didn't know what to do. If someone had rocked up with a gun and offered to take me into the garden and shoot me I would have accepted gratefully, but no one did so I sat there for a while with my head in my hands and cried a bit. Once I had gained enough composure to move Bob forwards and off Husband's car there was only one thing left to do. Ring Husband and spill my guts. The only saving grace was that I could tell him over the phone and not face to face to witness first hand what I knew would be the performance of his life. Biting the bullet I called his mobile. 'Hi, it's me,' I offered.

'Hello gorgeous, how's your birthday morning going?,' I could almost hear him smiling down the phone. Remember these were the days of young love when we still liked each other.

'Errrm, not that good actually. There's been an accident,' I started.

'Are you ok? Are you hurt? What happened? Shall I come home?' The panic in his voice was rising but I knew it was only out of concern for my safety. I had to get it off my chest and over and done with, I felt like I might be sick quite soon.

'There's no need to come home, I'm ok but 'I've crashed into a car. . .'

A PAUSE

. . . your car!'

Teeth clenched and eyes closed tight with my arm draped over my face. I waited.

SILENCE

'Are you there,' I asked tentatively.

'What do you mean you've crashed into my car?' He questioned. His voice loud and high pitched. It's a family trait on Husband's side that when anyone is fuming, positively seething their voice increases in pitch until they sound like they've been at the helium. At this point he certainly sounded like he'd had a good gulp of it. He continued, 'ARE YOU JOKING? HOW THE FUCK DID YOU MANAGE THAT?... **Blah blah** ... WHY ARE YOU SUCH A SHIT DRIVER? ... **Blah blah** ... IT'S BECAUSE YOU DON'T CONCENTRATE WHEN YOU'RE BEHIND THE WHEEL, ALWAYS TOO BUSY ON YOUR PHONE OR THINKING ABOUT OTHER THINGS ... **Blah blah** ...' He was raging mad and there wasn't a great deal I could say to diffuse the situation so I listened to him rant on and on and on whilst wincing into my sleeve.

He didn't speak to me for nearly a week for damaging his beloved car. He even cancelled the fancy restaurant he had booked for my birthday, leaving us sitting in the living room at opposite ends of the settee pretending not to look at each other. No one died that day so I'm not sure what all the fuss was about. His car was fine after a visit to the car hospital and Bob was tough as old boots and just needed a new bumper.

It was a few years later when Bob and I eventually parted ways when he was abducted from the tenfoot. I still feel bad about it because I didn't even realise he had been taken until 2 days later. I'd been catching the bus to work to avoid having to park in town in an effort to stop getting parking tickets. It wasn't until I was contacted by the police to confirm that I was the owner of Bob that I knew he was gone. He had been found not far from our house wrapped around a tree. The authorities explained it was joy riders and that he was now a right off and wouldn't be able to be repaired. At least he had a bit of fun during his last hours as a functioning vehicle.

This is when Hector (fourth car) made an appearance. The most modern car I'd ever had. A black Citroen Saxo with power steering, electric windows and not a manual choke in sight. I felt like I was driving around in a Lamborghini. The likelihood is that I probably did have a near miss in Hector at some time during his reign but I can't place it. He must be the only car I have owned that hasn't been pranged. Although I'm sure he had, I just can't remember. Don't get me wrong, his life was still as eventful as the others. He died because someone on Husband's building site drove a forklift truck into him so hard his bottom fell off, and before that he served as a bedroom for our dogs for a few weeks during one summer when we first moved to where we live now before we built our house.

Samantha the Monster Truck

Husband had a monster truck for a long time and has only recently sold her which was a bit of a wrench. We loved her. When people say that dogs look like their owners, well the same was true of Samantha. Who is Samantha? I hear you yell. She was our cool as fuck truck and was named by the children. She was jacked up so high the average Joe would not be able to scale her and get in unaided. She had huge tires that looked like they had once belonged to a tractor. She reeked of Husband. The only thing that could have made her more like Husband is if she had been covered in camo print. She was the transport that got me to hospital to birth my first Anklebiter (after having to be hoisted in, all that way up by a buckling Husband) and she was my day to day companion who ferried me and the Anklebiters around when they were very small because Husband had enlisted Hector the Saxo for work on the basis that he drank less petrol and that Samantha might be safer for the children. He was absolutely accurate about that anyway. There was no way there was any threat of being crushed to death in a potential collision when the cab was 9 ft off the floor and her wheels were bigger than most cars. I must admit the sheer power of driving Samantha went to my head. It made me feel invincible like no one could touch me and I did regularly run people off the road, not in a carjacking sort of a way but more in a bullying the other car back onto their own side of the road sort of a way. She was so big and scary looking no one wanted to tango with her.

I did once crash her a little bit into a railing at a zebra crossing which then forced my hand, giving me no other option than to lie to Husband about it. The traffic light was red and I took the opportunity to send a quick text. Although still very silly, this was before it was against the law. I think? I'm not entirely sure what happened but I know while I was stationary the truck was creeping forwards inch by inch. Probably a combination of a lack of handbrake and still being in gear, so when I'd finished on my phone and began to pull away Samantha lurched forward and into the railing next to the curb earning a huge scuff on the front bumper.

Shit shit shit.

Although Husband claimed he didn't check the truck after I had driven it, I knew he did. Given my track record with accidents and not overachieving at looking after the vehicles under my care I didn't blame him. He might have thought he was being covert but I spotted his eagle eyed once over's a mile off. It was after one of these routine secret, not so secret once over's, that I was questioned as to the acquisition of the front bumper scuff. It was unfortunate but he left me with no other option than to fabricate a story on the spot (which I'm lousy at because I'm a hopeless liar) which involved a 3 legged cat that had thrown itself into the middle of the road, forcing me to swerve into the railing to avoid being a cat killer. Back then it had the same amount of credibility as it does today. Husband called me out on this, so obviously I had to stick to my story and defend myself to the bitter end. It became a running joke. Anything that happened in day to day life that implied I was at fault in some way, Husband would randomly say, 'It won't be her fault, I bet a 3 legged cat jumped out in front of her.'

I could see his point.

Roy the BMW Estate

So, fast forward a few more years and picture this ...I had definitely come up in the world when we bought a BMW estate car just before my 30th birthday. He was old but in immaculate condition and I just felt generally fussy that at last I had a half decent car. His name was Roy. We hadn't had him for long when unfortunately one of his arms got ripped off. By arm, I am referring to the front passenger side door. I shit you not. It was an innocent accident that once again left me looking for a gunman in my garden or a door to door cyanide pill seller.

We were all in the car on our way out somewhere, I was driving, Husband was in the passenger seat and the Anklebiters in the back. We drove down our driveway from the house to the road which is long and narrow but very straight so if it becomes necessary to back up the driveway for any reason it's fairly easy to negotiate. This can be done at quite a speed and has been, frequently. As we reached the road Husband asked me to stop so he could check our post box. We have a couple of regular post people and they are both on the lazy side, cramming all sorts of crap that doesn't really fit into the box when it wouldn't be that much of a hardship to drive the extra 100 yards to the house, so we empty it each day to prevent all the junk mail backing up. I stopped, and he popped out to investigate the mountain of useless shit we had been left. Making the most of these extra few minutes I quickly logged in to my online banking on my phone to make a transfer, something I meant to do before we left the house but got sidetracked. If I left it any longer I'd definitely forget again. Just as I was completing the transfer I heard Husband shout that he'd forgotten his bank card at the house and we had to go back. Always one for a spot of multitasking I shouted back that I'd whip back for it. Without waiting for the response I chucked my phone onto the passenger seat, slung Roy into reverse whilst looking over my left shoulder so I could see the driveway through the back windscreen and put my foot down. Roy was nimble and moved quickly until nearly instantly the most almighty crashing sound ground us to a halt. Instinctively I covered my head and I could hear the children wailing. It suddenly occurred to me that something dreadful had happened. Had we been the victims of a carjacking? Had a bomb gone off?

No

I had reversed backwards at great speed with the passenger door still wide open. Narrowly missing Husband and causing him to jump for cover into a bush, the door had ripped entirely off on the heavy duty gate post.

OH HOLY MOTHER OF GOD

Without giving a blow by blow, gory account of the shockingly colourful language that ensued, or how Husband was the image of a hysterical madman thanks to his rage, it's suffice to say emotions were suitably frayed. There was an awful lot of crying going on, some by the children, but mostly by me, more from the shock I think. Once the waters had calmed and we had arranged for Roy to have a new arm I was positively steam rollered by the usual lectures regarding the following;

1. My blatant lack of care for anything that had the misfortune to have me in charge of it.

2. My total disregard for the value of money because I am not the main breadwinner and therefore apparently think Husband has a secret money tree growing in the back garden so I can break and destroy things at will with no real concern, knowing he will just buy new ones.

Today I have a beautiful Mini Countryman named King Julian, who the Anklebiters named after our favourite character out of the film Madagascar. I shower him with love, take special care when driving him and even clean him out occasionally. I don't want to jinx his boring little existence but so far there has been nothing to write home about, and that's just the way I like it.

Andy Suck on These

They say you attract what you are. It is therefore a concern to me that the majority of my friends are bat shit crazy bitches.

I am a woman's woman. By that I mean I am all for the sisterhood. I believe that all women should support each other without excuse or exception and that we should stand strongly together shoulder to shoulder looking out for each other at every opportunity. I think I subscribe to this concept partly because woman are fucking magnificent, but also because I am fiercely loyal, and on occasion this has been the cause of a number of marital ruckuses between Husband and I. I have been accused in the past of putting friendships before our marriage and I want to make it clear here and now that this is not the case. The problem is, I value my friends and will do all I can to be there for them when I am needed. If this brushes with my family responsibilities then I try hard to work it out so I can be available for both. It goes without saying, but I'll say it anyway, that family ALWAYS will be my priority but as is the case for many of us this could mean spreading ourselves too thin or burning the candle at both ends. However you wish to phrase it, sometimes it's just not possible without someone feeling their nose has been pushed out. I'm not a complete moron and have learnt over the years that sometimes it's not plausible to be the friend that is ready, willing and available 24/7 for birthday drinks, hen weekends away, shopping trips or midnight emergencies, although I do my best. I am lucky enough, or have chosen well enough, that the majority of my small circle of buddies understand this and expect very little from our friendships, sometimes going without any contact for months. With this in mind it is never any different when we do get together again which only reinforces my ideals of what real friendship looks like.

Friends, partners in crime, confidents, cronies, cheerleaders, whatever you choose to call them, mine are the ones who ...

1. Are the random group of women you see on the dance floor when no one else is, wildly reenacting iconic dance moves

from the 80's like no one is watching. Sometimes roping in innocent passers by without an ounce of shame.

2. During a routine shopping trip, openly fart, loudly blame you then do a pump dance through the smell which is mainly celebratory but also is an excellent solution in dispersing the whiff.

3. Have a special sign language to privately communicate with each other in front of customers when in their hair salon mainly because they are ripping the piss out of actual paying clients.

4. Get 99% of their repeat custom of said clients because they are funny and always have a story to tell.

5. Think it's amusing to deliberately mispronounce YSL touche eclat extremely loudly whilst in the makeup section in Harvy Nicks so it sounds more like they are shouting about touching their clit. *As in clitorus, and yes, it was during a girls cocktail afternoon.*

6. Openly mock the Actor who plays Andy Sugden from Emmerdale on a night out in Leeds by repeatedly asking him when the last bus to Hotten was, in every ... single ... pub. **This happened, and led to police intervention and a restraining order . . . It actually never but it easily could have done.**

The weekend away had been planned to coincide with one of our quieter friends' birthdays. Leeds had been nominated for the place we would be let loose so we had booked a hotel, meaning we wouldn't have to negotiate the last train home once under the influence of a few too many cocktails, **or cock and tails as some of my cronies like to call them. You can't buy class.** We had played the train game before on a previous trip and unfortunately it had resulted in only half our party returning to our own home town safely, the other half had somehow managed to board the wrong train and arrived safely in another town that was nowhere near their home. This saw one of their long suffering, understandably grumpy husbands have to tackle a 60 mile round trip at 2am to collect and deliver home the rowdy bunch. Not ideal.

Being larger than our town, and the hub of anything alternative and unusual , Leeds was buzzing with activity. The pubs and bars were far superior and much more glitzy than our local ones, just what we were looking for. After arriving on the train into Leeds station all present and correct, no one missing this time around, we made our way to the hotel to dump the bags, put some heels and lippy on and plan our evening. Being friends with a couple of hairdressers you'd think you might be able to weadle a free hair spruce before a night on the tiles but the best I could expect was a horrendous poodle do, thanks to the carmen rollers that once belonged to my grandma, **yes, that's how old they were,** and in the hands of a hairdresser whose only goal was a laugh at my expense, the outcome wasn't pretty. To be fair I should have counted my chickens that with the ancient wiring they hadn't caught fire and blown my head off. Transforming my long, shoulder length hair into a tightly curled bob/mullet type affair that was now chin length, I looked a bugger, much to the complete delight of the hairdressers. There had been a few little vodkas consumed on the train ride so this may have encouraged the devilment and lubricated the belly laughs a little. I'm not against a spot of mischief and am only too happy to laugh at myself, and what a good job. Eventually making it out of the hotel, the girls, me and my ridiculous hair headed for the first bar.

We drank vodka, Mojitos and our old friend Jack like they were going out of fashion. We danced our socks off amongst the crowds, showcasing some rather impressive moves, more specifically the one where you pretend to slap the face of your partner but they move their face to each side as you perform the dramatic slap, a very accomplished manoeuvre and probably not one that should be done on an innocent passerby, mostly because the likelihood of them thinking they are being attacked as opposed to being part of a dance routine is quite high.

A couple of hours in and the night was going well. The drinks were flowing and the laughs had been present in sackfuls. Our quieter friend seemed to be enjoying herself, only making herself scarce at a few crucial points when the others were being overly embarrassing. We were waiting for our drinks at the crowded bar and chattering about something silly when I could see that one of the hairdressers had been distracted by something, a smile spreading slowly across her face. One of the others had also noticed. 'What are you gawping at?' She shouted to the hairdresser over the thump of the music.

'Andy Sugden is standing behind you,' Replied the hairdresser, nodding over our friend's shoulder.

'Andy Sugden? Why do I know that name? Is it someone we know?' She shouted back.

'Emmerdale Farm Andy Sugden,' Said the hairdresser, as if by way of an explanation.

Emmerdale. A popular English soap opera set in the heart of the Yorkshire Dales which is also the village the residents of the program live in. Primarily made up of farms and small holdings, the nearest town for shopping or anything other than sheep, pigs and more sheep is Hotten. In the program there's usually a scene at the bus stop or some sort of reference to going into, or getting back from Hotten.

She wasn't wrong. The actor who played Andy Sugden was indeed standing just behind us. A brooding, moody character in the program he didn't look that much different in real life. He actually didn't look like he was having much fun at all. You'd think this might deter our hairdresser friend but it never. She squeezed by a couple of us, and approached Andy Sugden. Her face deadpan and serious, she tapped him on the shoulder to get his full attention, brazenly interrupting his conversation and said, 'Excuse me, could you tell me when the last bus to Hotten is please?' He held her gaze for a few seconds as if contemplating his response then without any reaction at all turned his back on her and continued his conversation. Honestly this was his first mistake. Had he told her it would be due in half an hour and played her game I'm positive she would have been happy with this and left it at that, but that never happened. Instead she continued, 'Please, I really need to know, I've got to be home soon, I've got an early morning tomorrow, it's lambing season, you should know that.'

She followed this statement with a frenzied giggle, looking at the rest of our gang for support and they didn't let her down. Our quieter friend and I looked on in horror as this developed into a full blown group activity that would have easily landed any of them a part in Emmerdale for their acting skills. They were clearly in their element but after a little gentle persuasion from me we quickly finished our drinks and moved on to the next pub. Thank God. And thank god we never ran into him in any other pubs.

Except we did.

We managed to run into him a further 3 times in different bars and each time the events that ensued all took a similar format. He would be asked when the last bus to Hotten was by our group of hysterically laughing women that were becoming more shit faced by the minute. He would either ignore us, or politely say he didn't know, on one occasion I distinctly heard him say 'Oh for fuck sake,' before stalking off. It seemed this joke was not going to lose its appeal and his blatant annoyance about the whole thing was making the situation worse, totally encouraging them. In the last place that we saw him, one of the girls decided she'd quite like a photo with him. This was before the days when everyone had cameras on their phones and instead relied on small awkward digital cameras. Clumsily dragging her top of the range one out of her clutch, spilling most of the other contents onto the floor she waved it in poor Andy's face before linking arms with him so he couldn't escape and handing the camera to one of the hairdressers to play photographer. Really playing the part, the hairdresser started to give direction to the subjects like a photography professional, telling them to 'pout', and 'work that smile' and say 'cheeeeese' and 'boooobs' and other random stuff she hoped would embarrass and irritate him no doubt.

Just at the point when the photograph should have been taken, Andy calmly leaned forwards and reached towards the camera, turning it round to face the way it should be in order to take a photo. It appeared the 26 mojitos **or thereabouts** had taken effect on our hairdresser and had provoked temporary alcohol related blindness causing her to look down the lens instead of the eye hole. **I'll be damned if I have the faintest idea what the real term is for the 'eye hole' on a camera.** Still showing no emotion he then moved back to his given position and waited patiently for the hairdresser to finish the photo shoot.

That was the last instalment of the night that involved Andy Sugden, or 'Andy suck on these' as he was renamed later on in the night by our quiet friend who had emerged from her quietness like a beautiful butterfly from a cocoon, if butterflies were drunk and obscene. His new name came about for a combination of reasons.

1. When you are irretrievably smashed and slurring and trying to say Andy Sugden it can very occasionally, but not very often, sound slightly, **but not much,** like 'Andy Suck on These'

2. Once back at the hotel in the small hours we used room service to order some food, someone got a panini that should have come with salad but clearly the hotel kitchen had run out, so instead had sliced up approximately 8 large tomatoes as garnish, which although is categorically not funny in any way shape or form, was totally hilarious when you are 3 sheets to the wind and don't know what planet you're on. It also lent itself very nicely to 'Andy suck on these ...tomatoes'. **I'm sorry, I am acutely aware none of this is funny unless you've had 26 mojitos or 12 bottles of**

wine. Maybe go off and have a little drink and then come back and start from the beginning.

I'm desperately trying to think of something that can be taken from this experience but I'm failing miserably. The key messages here I think are. . .

1. Try not to verbally abuse anyone, especially if they are famous and in a soap opera.

2. Do not drink 26 Mojitos in one night because it is a recipe for disaster and may give you temporary blindness. This will be followed by a mean case of the spins and eventual retching and consequent spewing.

3. Do not attempt to catch the last train home when a cocktail has been consumed because you'll end up at the wrong end of the country to where you live, you'll be in the doghouse for at least a week and your husband will do his best to drag this out for as long as possible. Not from this particular tale strictly

speaking but important enough to mention I think.

And something which is paramount generally in life ...

    4.   Don't be a Cunt.

'I now Pronounce you Husband and Shit Machine'

A few years ago I was lucky enough to be asked to be a bridesmaid. My friend and her Fiance were planning their wedding abroad and after exhausting a few different options settled for Greece.

It was booked a year in advance and that year was full of important decisions. She had cleverly delegated the whole bridesmaid operation to the bridesmaids, absolving herself from any kind of responsibility as to what we would wear and what we would look like. Even down to the colour. I was one of four, thirty somethings, desperate to look demure, and not to let her down. There was one bridesmaid in particular that took the lead, subtly asserting authority over the rest of us, as so often happens when groups are left to their own devices. I for one was thankful that her natural leadership skills had shone through, vindicating me of any responsibility (or blame) whatsoever.

And that's how I ended up in a canary yellow ball gown, looking a little too much like 'Fat Fairy' from Willow the Wisp.

There had been a final choice of two. The first one was perfect if you were a size 6 and ate nothing at all for three days prior to wearing it. A very pretty one shouldered little number that was as tight as cling film. Not really a feasible option for me. The second was more forgiving, low cut and free flowing. Something that Aphrodite would have been proud of. Definitely more my thing.

Bridesmaid dress under my belt, all that was left for me to do was organise the children to be away from home for four days. Sounds easy doesn't it? Preparing them for every possible eventuality that could happen in 4 days including but not limited to outfits, gaming consoles, school uniforms, school projects, paints, favourite socks **WTF?**, favourite teddies, favourite snacks (of course they don't taste the same when grandma buys exactly the same thing from exactly the same shop), the list goes on. Logistically, trying to organise the back and forths between two sets of grandparents, another grandad, and an auntie was a nightmare. Not to mention the friend's house they were going to. According to our 10 year old , it was a matter of life and death and could only happen on that exact day during the only 4 days we were out of the country. Obviously.

Dress sorted.

Children sorted.

Just one more thing before we could jet off into the sunset. Probably the most stressful challenge so far. Husband's outfit. For those of you who know and love Husband on a personal level, I'm sure you'll agree he's not what you'd call an easy man. He's the sort that would argue black is white, hot is cold, up is down, red is green and that John Seanor is probably a woman. I think you get the idea. He's the sort of man that will ask my opinion on which shoe or trainer matches his jeans the best. As I pay close attention to him turning each way for a few seconds so I can get the full benefit of each shoe, I know with certainty that when I give my answer he will absolutely always choose the opposite.

A few weeks before we were due to fly, I inquired as to what he thought he might wear for the wedding, to which he replied 'a wetsuit'. After that I decided it was best to leave him to it. After all, I'm not his mother. He's a man in his forties, old enough to wear what he liked. I would look lovely in canary yellow and he would at least be there with me, wearing God only knows what, but still he would be there, helping celebrate our friends' nuptials. A week before we left for Greece we had met with the bride and groom for drinks. My friend who has known Husband as long as I have and knows what he can be like, had taken the opportunity to mention that she knew he didn't like dressing up and he would be more than welcome to attend the ceremony in bermuda shorts and a wife beater. *I'm almost positive everyone knows that a wife beater is a white vest usually seen on middle aged men partial to a tinnie.* Cunning. Devious. I liked her style.

Challenge him to do exactly as he wanted and he would almost definitely do the opposite.

As the last bits were going into the case I noticed a smart pair of navy blue chino shorts and a linen shirt.

Husband's outfit sorted.

The Day of Departure

The flight was four hours long. We had eaten a nice meal in the airport and used the ablutions. Everyone knows that it's best to try and avoid the cramped smelly chemical toilets onboard the flight that no one ever flushes. Husband always commandeers the window seat when we fly so as not to run the risk of having to exchange pleasantries with anyone he doesn't know. This left me with a middle seat. To my left in the aisle seat was an elderly lady who, as luck would have it, I got on famously with. From the second she sat down we never stopped talking. Other than the occasional toilet trip (for her, not me, I knew better) and the intermittent exchange of murray mints and werther's original, it seemed like we didnt come up for air until the pilot announced to belt up for landing. The incessant chatter between my new best pal and I was starting to grate a little on Husband, I could tell. An eye roll was definitely brewing. Husband isn't a keen flyer, not that he's scared, maybe only scared he might die of boredom. For this reason he refuses to fly anywhere that takes longer than 4 hours. One year I lied a little bit about how long it took to get to Egypt. I told him it was the customary 4 hours, not 6. I also may have neglected to mention that we had to pick up passengers in Gatwick. That particular holiday I came close to being sold for 6 camels. I'm not even joking.

The hotel was opulent, our room was beautiful and the climate didn't disappoint, still around 20 degrees at just after 10pm. Our room had two bedrooms, two bathrooms, robes, slippers and all the free shower gel you could ever want. Overlooking the pool, it had a spacious balcony and views out to sea. I was glad I'd booked the executive room. I had texted my friend earlier from the taxi on the way over to let her know we would be arriving shortly. They had flown out a few days beforehand to make some last minute wedding preparations and to top up their tans. I had got as far as opening my suitcase while Husband checked out the balcony when there was a knock at the door.

   The door swung open. It was so lovely to see our friends. There were a few excited squeals and lots of hugging and hand shaking. Husband took 'Husband to be' outside to show off the balcony while us women caught up on all the essentials

- Did the mini bar contain wine?
- How much wine?
- Which dresses had been packed for the holiday?
- Was it acceptable to wear spanx under wedding and bridesmaid dresses? Etc etc.

Looking through the glass sliding door onto the balcony I could see the Husbands were having a beer and becoming quite animated in their discussions.

Another knock at the door. My friend and I looked at each other, puzzled. Who could it be? The other guests weren't due to arrive until the following day and it couldn't be housekeeping, it was 10 o'clock at night! So who was it? The Husbands had also heard the knock and had come back inside, curious to see who was there. I answered the door.
'Hotel security,' said the strapping Greek man standing on the other side of the door, looking like he'd just come straight from his stripper job.

'We've had complaints about the noise coming from this room.' The look of shock must have been plastered on our faces. He continued, 'It's very late and we enforce a strict no noise policy after 10pm.' Now I admit Husband does have one of those voices that carries. When he's on the phone he's so loud he doesn't necessarily need the actual phone because you can hear him for miles around. He also gets mistaken for a Geordie quite a lot which is weird but the only thing I can reference it to is how they sound on Auf Wiedersehen Pet. Loud and Geordieish. The point I'm making here is that we had been in the room for precisely 8.5 minutes. Husband had not been on the phone once in that time and we hadn't been quick enough to trash the place so who was making the noise? We learned very quickly after that incident on the first night that noise in this hotel was very much frowned upon. Forbidden in fact. Not ideal when you're there for a wedding celebration, and not ideal when you are married to Husband. Just to be clear by noise I mean anything above a whisper. When we checked in, reception should have said, 'Hello and welcome to our hotel. Do not make noise, do not have fun and under no circumstances shall you laugh on your balcony or we will have no choice but to send round a stripper posing as a security guard to arrest you.' At least then we would have known the rules.

The next couple of days floated by without incident and were filled with delicious food, lots of lounging, lots of sun, and lots of quiet. We had met all of the wedding party at this point which was made up of parents, brothers, sisters and friends. Everyone got along great and everything was going to plan. One night we stumbled on a karaoke bar. It was not associated with the hotel and was off site so we could speak normally. We could even sing, shout, and scream if we had wanted to just for the hell of it. We didn't actually do any of those things but after a few beers there was an extremely convincing dance impression of Leroy from 'Fame', specifically, some high leg kicks, executed beautifully by Husband

The Wedding Day
The morning of the wedding was finally here. Not scheduled to tie the knot until later on in the afternoon the morning was free for the bride and I to do lots of nice things. I was the only bridesmaid staying at the hotel so it was

just us, the gruesome twosome. I had planned full body massages for us both followed by a few hours round the pool soaking up the sun. What could be a more perfect start to the day you begin married life. The boys of the wedding party, mainly friends and a brother of the Husband to be, had all got ready ridiculously early and had planned to relax with a few drinks and a game of crazy golf. Crazy, quiet golf as the course was on site at the hotel. Husband had been enrolled as nanny so was super busy dutifully helping with keeping the beer flowing, tying windsor knots and generally keeping everyone on track (and out of prison).

Standing outside the spa on the ground floor sporting my hotel robe and slippers I saw the bride approaching. Why was she fully clothed? She sheepishly informed me that although it was a kind gesture she couldn't bear it if random people had to touch her and that it gave her the creeps. Fair enough. So I went on my own to have what turned out to be the most painful full body massage of my life. Afterwards, I felt like a bus had mowed me down and then reversed back over me. Not exactly what I was looking for. Not relaxing at all. I was actually glad that the bride had bailed on me because if she had gone through with it, it would have ruined her day and I would have been solely responsible for her walking down the aisle like The Hunchback of Notre Dame. Given that the first part of my plan had failed miserably I was eager to get on with the next phase. I wrestled myself into my blue flamingo bikini and was ready on my sunbed, a bit surprised the bride wasn't there already. Scrolling through my playlists on my phone trying to decide what to listen to, my friend's name popped up onto the screen. A text message.

Bride: Something's happened. I can't come.

Me: What's happened? Are you ok?

Nothing. No response. I dialled her number and waited. It rang for a very long time before the line picked up. I was greeted by breathless sobs coming thick and fast. 'What's happened?' I demanded. 'Are you ok?' Nothing except sobs. 'Where are you? Tell me and I'll come and get you,' I explained calmly.

'No! NO! Don't come. I'm on the third floor back stairs and I've poo'd myself!' She wailed almost hysterically. 'It's everywhere and I don't know what to do! It's on the floor and in my bikini and just as it happened the maid from housekeeping walked onto the stairwell and saw everything!'

At this point I couldn't help but laugh. Not the quiet kind that was allowed in this place but a monstrous cackle that was heard by the whole pool area. At least I presume that's why they were all gawping. I admit it, I am a bad friend. What can I say? It was VERY funny. This was only surpassed when I later found out that in order to make it back to her room on the 7th floor she had fashioned her sarong into a makeshift nappy to catch the shit and prevent any further damage to hotel property. Desperate to go again and only making it back to her room by the skin of her teeth, she whipped off the sarong for quick access and fired shit straight up the wall and all over the WHOLE bathroom.

It was the best day of my life.

Humiliation and I usually walked hand in hand together down the bumpy road of life so it was a novelty for me to not be holding the shitty end of the stick (or the sarong) for once.

Once I had regained my composure, still on the phone we managed to converse just enough to agree that she would clean up as best she could then bring her stuff to my room. The original plan had been for all the bridesmaids to meet in the brides room and have a lovely time quaffing champagne and getting ready together. Unfortunately after the events that had just taken place that was no longer possible. Her room (and her whole floor she told me) now smelt like a farm. The bathroom was in such a mess she didn't know if she should call housekeeping or just burn it down.

The rest of the day ran smoothly. We had managed to have a nice time getting ready, slightly rushed after what had just unfolded but we were together and had assured the bride that it happens to the best of us.

The place that had been chosen for the wedding was absolutely breathtaking. A real winner. Sea views as far as the eye could see and inside the Greek structure where the vows would take place was a really pretty inside outside courtyard that had been decorated beautifully. The boys were already in position and the guests were waiting eagerly to see the blushing bride. Definitely blushing for good reason, other than being a bride, but no one else knew that. Not yet anyway. As we waited outside the entrance for the photographer to make our entrance, passers-by, locals and tourists alike were waving to us. Apparently everyone loves a wedding. We felt like celebrities.

The ceremony went well, and without incident. Everyone was over the moon and there was excitement in the air. In Greece it is customary for there to be the registrar who marries the couple, a translator and the Mayor present. It was soon very clear, and much to the amusement of the bride and her maids that the Mayor only had eyes for the groom and was unashamedly chatting him up whilst completely ignoring everyone else. He wasn't cooperating with the registrar as much as he should have been because he was too engrossed in trying to make the groom his new boyfriend! There were times when it was unclear who was marrying who. The bride and groom or the groom and the Mayor!

The whole wedding party celebrated long into the night. There was mouthwatering food, wedding cake and lots to drink. There were a few early disappearances and rumours of skinny dipping. Not substantiated. The bride and groom had been too shy to dance the first dance so Husband had obliged. Thankfully he had re-thought the wetsuit and was looking handsome in his linen shirt and shorts. Swinging round one of the groom's merry men, Husband took the lead and danced his socks off, they made a lovely couple.

The mood was jovial and I think I speak for all who attended when I say that we felt honoured to have been invited to share such a special day. More importantly my friend now had the best wedding story ever, and I knew she would never tell it. So I have.

I've only been Kidnapped Twice (but only one turned into a hostage situation)

One New Year before Husband and I had succumbed to the Anklebiters we decided to have a fortnight in Egypt. I sold the idea of Egypt to him with stories of the hot climate, striking sunsets and partly by lying about the flight time. Husband is severely allergic to flying anywhere that takes longer than 4 hours. It bores him, and when bored he morphs into the MOST annoying man on the planet. It's not pretty. It was actually a 5 hour flight but would take 6 as we had to stop in London to collect passengers after departing from Manchester. I had made a strategic decision and decided to omit these small details. He would have refused outright to go and I would have french kissed goodbye to my Middle Eastern dream. My reasoning was that once onboard it would be too late to back out and too inappropriate to throw a massive tantrum. Not a fan of public humiliation, once this came to his attention he would most likely choose to throw a few mucky looks in my direction whilst systematically pretending I didn't exist. That I could cope with. He'd get over it hopefully by the time we arrived, ready to enjoy our holiday.

We booked bed and breakfast at a posh hotel which turned out to be the most luxurious one we'd ever stayed in. It was truly plush and very swanky. Our room was a Deluxe Seaview with a balcony, perfect for lounging and snoozing in the midday sun. Breakfast was undeniably our best part of the day. Both being 'greedies' it was sometimes a four hour affair, or at least it felt that way. With such a selection it would have been rude not to sample everything on offer. After exotic fruits and yoghurt to line the stomach, we would move on to the omelette counter. Yes, an omelette counter. Where a little man stood patiently at a little hob behind a little counter and literally cooked whatever you wanted in front of you. With about 27000 different ingredients it was tricky to decide what to have and sometimes it was unavoidable to go back 3 or 4 times. It was essential though that enough space was left for the hundreds of sweet pastries and breads that taunted us the whole way through our attempt at the longest breakfast sitting the world had ever seen. Sometimes I'd take a bag to smuggle out some of my favourite stuff, much to Husband's utter disgust. Not a fan of any type of poggy behaviour, he was always very anxious not to appear to be a tramp by stealing food that he had already paid for. I know, try and work that one out if you can.

The staff were wonderful, nothing was too much trouble for them and if we slipped them the equivalent of 20p they literally did anything we asked. Polishing our sunglasses and bringing drinks, eagerly watching until we put down our empties so they could race to replace them. Husband, always a good tipper, had struck up some sort of an agreement with one of the members of staff at the beginning of the holiday whereby our towels would be put on the best sunbeds around the pool each morning. Thus avoiding the mad Germans running to steal the best places at 5am, without us ever having to get out of bed. And, that was for the cheap as cheesy chips, bargain price of £2 total. I bet there was nothing they wouldn't do for £2. There's no doubt in my mind that they would have carried out an assasination on a target of our choice and then brought the corpse to eat our evening meal with us, if we had requested it. *Sorry, I've been watching some fairly disturbing old school horror of late. I don't know why because I hate being scared and hate horror films.* I feel I'm drifting from the point here. Point being they were very attentive and extremely good at their job.

There were 3 different swimming pools to choose from and a lazy river. Generally we used the adult pools, not yet having our own kiddies. We weren't overly keen on listening to everyone else's, although that said there weren't very many kids around at the time we were there. I'd ventured onto the lazy river one ill fated day. The episode that ensued is not something I remember fondly however it is also one of Husbands best memories to date so he tells me. Gently floating with the current around the river I could see a commotion up ahead. There was a lady at the edge of the pool frantically gesturing to me, beckoning me to go to her. She was shouting but the noise from the rushing water was too loud and I couldn't make out what she was saying. Husband then appeared next to the lady, deep in concentration as she was explaining something to him. Halfway through he started to gesture to me as well. I started to make my way slowly over to one of the ladders and as I did I shouted 'Is everything ok?' Her face was thunderous but what was wrong with Husband? He was openly laughing then held up his palms at me as if telling me to stop. What on earth was going on? 'I'm coming, I'll be there in a minute.' As I spoke his laughter increased. By the time I made it to the edge of the pool Husband was a hopeless mess, laughing so hard he couldn't speak. It was left to the lady to explain to me that her 10 year old son had accidentally taken a massive shit in the pool and they were quickly trying to evacuate it to prevent anyone getting poisoned. By this time Husband had recovered enough to gleefully tell me that as I was swimming over to the edge, I was in the turds' direct path and could have easily swallowed it at any given moment when I was shouting. Best day of his life. Horrid man. And as for the lazy river shitter, what 10 year old does that? And how does anyone expel something comparable to a tortoise's head in a swimming pool without knowing? All excellent questions.

In addition to obsessively having our sunglasses cleaned, drinking ourselves to death, planning assassinations for £2 a go and trying hard not to eat pool poo, we also went snorkeling. The sea was amazing. Clear, crisp and packed full of brightly coloured, strange looking fish. Not really one for getting my face wet, it was a little out of my comfort zone at first but I persevered and I'd like to think I even made Husband fairly proud, until a small fish I was looking at bared its teeth at me. Not in a particularly fierce way like I imagine a piranha would, but more in the way like it had stolen a set of false teeth and was about to break into song. Anyway I just about cacked my bikini and had to be escorted from the water. Husband enjoyed water sports very much and took the opportunity to go swim chasing stingrays and sharks and other super dangerous Bond film worthy type creatures. All I can say is that it's one thing to be watching a shark and know without doubt it's a shark. It's quite another to be watching a beautiful elegant pale pink glittery little fish that out of nowhere starts impersonating Simon Cowel. It put me right off doing anything that involved getting my hair or face wet again. I knew there was a method to my madness. There is an inbuilt reason I do not get wet above the neck and that is because when I do, bad things happen. To further illustrate this point, years later I found myself in a water park in Turkey with Husband, the Anklebiters who were very small at the time, and our grown up girls. They had persuaded me, and obviously what I mean by persuaded, is tricked me, into going on the most God awful death trap of a waterslide of all time. Always attempting to make me show myself up in one way or another, purely for their own personal amusement, they had won and I had accepted their challenge. Only having 2 hands and needing to hold my nose, hold my sunglasses on my face and hold onto my bikini I was acutely aware just a little too late that it was going to end badly. And it did. By the time I reached the bottom of the horror that was masquerading as a fun corkscrew slide I had lost my glasses, lost my bikini bottoms and could be found screaming my head off in the overflow pool at the bottom. More out of shock than for the help I knew would never arrive.

The lessons here are;

1. Aways trust your instincts

2.Never trust your older children when they have that all too familiar glint in their eye.

3.Always make sure you are Brazilian ready downstairs because you never know when you will be involved in a freak watersliding accident. I was not Brazilian ready, and for what I know was undoubtedly longer than a split second my 70s porn star bush was out and proud for all to see.

Back to Egypt.

On some nights we decided to venture out of the safety of the hotel and brave it amongst legitimate Egyptian people and their eateries. It didn't seem like braving it at the time, it's only really when I look back on it now that I realise just how authentic it actually was and we were perhaps silently begging to be mugged or worse. Bimbling down the hustle and bustle of the strip surrounded by shisha smoke and snake charmers music it was a place that felt extremely alluring and romantic. A different feeling altogether than when you do a fortnight in Benidorm.

This particular night in question Husband and I weren't talking. Unsure now all these years later what we had barnied over it's true to say he was giving me the cold shoulder, and even colder stares between the dirty looks. He had jumped on the hotel shuttle in an effort to escape me, following a heated debate over something. But why should he get to escape? So I went with him, totally ruining his storm off power. By the time we got off at the strip his anger had not eased, not one little bit. He swiftly stormed off down the strip, trying his best to accelerate away from me and there I was trying to keep up by doing a very uncool half run shuffle thing. This was the exact perfectly timed moment that we were approached by a young girl of around 15 or 16. She was clutching some kind of paperwork and as she found her stride chatting away in near perfect English I realised she was telling us about disabled Egyption children and how we could help. As I write this it is totally obvious we were about to be done over but at the time it wasnt. Honestly. Always a sucker for anyone or anything in need, she had my full attention. Husband wasn't convinced because he isn't a pushover like me and never takes any crap off anyone but surprisingly he let her speak and seemed to listen. Before we knew it she was leading us to her parents' shop so we could sign up to help a child with no arms or legs or face, or something equally horrific. On route we had even looked at each other a few times with sadness and with a look that said 'let's not fight anymore because there are children out there with no arms, legs or faces'. The narrow alley we were walking down was very quiet and there were hardly any people around unlike the constant throb of the strip we'd just come from. As we were led into the shop it was painfully clear something wasn't right when the door was locked behind us, the young girl disappeared into the back and out came 4 heavies. It soon became apparent we had been taken under false pretences to what appeared to be a homemade perfume shop. Having perfume bottles roughly shoved under our noses and gestures made about money right in our faces was not pleasant and if I'm being honest was bloody scary. What they had no way of knowing was that Husband himself was a weapon. A force to be reckoned with on a good day, a bad day or any other fucking day. It was only a matter of time before the Hulk appeared. True to form, all it took was a small amount of aggression from one of the heavies. Raising his voice and roughly pushing a perfume bottle at us when Husband snapped. Shouting and bawling, arms waving, squaring up to all 4 of the heavies, going absolutely crazy horse, Husband came into his own. By now 9 foot tall with protruding veins in his neck and head (the usual drill) he looked like an escaped crazed lunatic. The heavies must have also shared this view because suddenly they were eager to unlock the door and release us.

The Hulk - 1
The Heavies - Nil

Due to the relief of escaping unscathed, without being tied up or tortured, my euphoria was high and it was because of this it took me a while to realise that Husband was still as mad as a raging bull, even once we got back to the strip. Already cross at me for something I can't even remember, it occurred to me that I was now shouldering the whole blame for the small kidnapping incident that had just taken place. It was just then that a leary old Egyptian man with impeccable timing shouted at Husband 'I geeve 6 camels for your beauuutiful woman.' I could feel the creepiness in his gaze prickling my neck. And why was he only offering 6 camels? To my knowledge that was the camel exchange rate to trade a tin of beans or an old flea bitten hat, or similar.

    Husband didn't miss a beat. 'Take her for free. She's yours!' He stalked off into the night once again trying to lose me. That evening we didn't make up. We didn't stroll hand in hand amongst the authentic smells and sounds of the real Egypt, but we did manage to survive a kidnapping ordeal and I had managed to dodge being sold for a miserable amount of camels. All in all it wasn't the worst thing that had ever happened.

You'd think after this near miss that we'd be more switched on to these antics. If you did think that you'd be giving us too much credit. 10 years, 1 Anklebiter, a bump and a wedding later we were honeymooning in Marrakesh. 2 year old Anklebiter was at home with Grandma so we could have 4 nights of fascinating culture. We had chosen to stay in a carefully selected, ancient Riad. A large traditional house built around a courtyard often converted into a swanky hotel by definition. The brochure had told me that ours was just over 200 years old and had been lovingly restored. We booked the King's suite. It looked and sounded perfect. The ideal combination of old world charm, romance and luxury. It was highly unfortunate however that the brochure did not include what the Riad or Kings Suit might smell like. I can tell you now, I'm fairly certain that the bedding, cushions, curtains and all other soft furnishings were most likely the ones that the King himself picked out 200 years ago and that was also the last time they saw a washing machine, or a can of febreeze. This wasn't helped by the fact I was 4 months pregnant and could smell everything within a 10 mile radius including the entire contents of the fridge in the room next door. This aside, Morocco was a mesmerising place. The local butcher had a spot just outside the front door of our Riad ruthlessly chopping off the heads of goats and chickens creating a steady stream of blood which ran down the street. Always one to embrace different cultures, this still unnerved me slightly. The daytimes were out of this world. An array of fabulous colours and smells, the markets left us speechless. It was like nothing we'd ever seen before. Imagine Aladdin's cave full of treasure and trinkets but on the scale of a football pitch, all the little stalls and cubby holes bursting with abundance, all linked together through a series of tunnels and tiny covered streets. The nights however, were a different ball game. For me anyway. I could blame my hormones for being on high alert and wanting to protect my bump from anything untoward but I can't be sure it was that. Come nightfall the place really came to life. It was so busy in the streets that we could barely see where we were standing. There were people in front, behind and to the sides of us. I felt like it was difficult to breathe. The streets overflowed with crowds of men standing on corners, outside of shops and generally congregating in huge gangs. There were few women because of the nature of their culture so it was predominantly men everywhere. Men in traditional dress, men in hats, men in uniform, men with guns. There was a strong military presence and it all put me on edge.

The second night we were on the hunt for somewhere to eat. Fighting our way through the hoards, a friendly face appeared and enquired if we were enjoying our stay at the Riad. Husband and I both looked at each other, our faces expressionless, it was clear neither of us had the faintest idea of who he was. He seemed to know us though, being overly friendly he was asking what we had planned over the next few days and talking about the wonderful food our Riad served. He then asked where we were planning on eating that night. The look of surprise on our faces was evidently a green flag to him as he proceeded to tell us about the loveliest little place that prepared the most delicious food. By now I had assumed our new best pal worked at our Riad. How else would he know us? And what a nice man to go out of his way to not only recommend a place to eat but to actually take us there. I looked at Husband, he reluctantly gave me the go ahead with an eye roll so we followed this guy. We walked and walked for a long time. The crowds had dispersed and it seemed that the few people that were still milling around were heading in the opposite direction. Husband had been giving me secret death stares for quite some time now, which I had chosen to ignore but it was too much for him. 'Where are we actually going?' He questioned irritably.

'To my house.' Replied our new best friend, smiling broadly.

'What?' Boomed Husband. Oh no, I could see the Hulk hovering just beneath the surface.

'My wife is a beautiful cook and smaller money than restaurants.' He informed us eagerly, like he was doing us a huge favour. For the love of God. Do we have a monstrous sign pinned to our backs saying ' Rip us off please, we are an easy target?' I'm thinking Yes we did.

'No I don't think so,' muttered Husband as we came to an abrupt halt. Turning on his heel, Husband grabbed my hand and stalked off back in the direction of the activity, dragging me behind, once again making me do the odd half run shuffle thing to keep up. Thankfully The Hulk never made an appearance that night. He must have known there was no immediate threat of death and let Husband handle it.

And that was the second time in my life I was kidnapped. At least this time we managed to avoid a hostage situation like in Egypt. Clearly we are getting better at this. I don't think you'll be surprised to learn that I have since been stripped of all my decision making responsibilities whilst on any holiday, especially when it involves-

1. Speaking to locals

2. Speaking to people
3. Speaking to stray dogs and headless goats.
4. Speaking to anyone or anything living or dead.

A Bat out of Hell will be gone when the morning comes. Hopefully

Each year, usually towards the end of summer, Husband abandons the Mothership and clears off for a few days with his pals to attend a carefully selected MotoGP race meet. Usually abroad, somewhere exciting like Italy or Eastern Europe but occasionally closer to home at venues as equally iconic like Donington Park or Silverstone. In all honesty, from the outside looking in it does not appear to be very enjoyable. With a selection of locations such as these I would have thought that a nice little hotel or privately rented apartment right amongst the action might be a good choice, especially since Husband and the other members of the posse who tend to frequent this trip are not spring chickens. Each year I stupidly assume that they are past their club 18-30 days of shitty accommodation and 24-7 drinking and that they might book something decent for a change. But they never do.

Husband isn't generally accustomed to 'roughing it' anymore, he likes nice things and under usual circumstances would put a stop to anything that involved anything else, but it's like he loses all rational thought where this trip is concerned. He allows his pals to book overnight arrangements at sub standard hostels and in weird old school buildings that don't look suitable to sleep in at all. After his trips he comes home with far fetched stories of total abandonment of the chosen craphole accommodation and tales of sleeping in a ditch at the race site, in a sleeping bag which someone weed on during an all night rave. I mean WTF? Does any of that sound enjoyable?

An avid fan of motorbikes and motorbike racing alike, it's not often he misses this annual jolly. It has become an unspoken understanding that during his time away things will go wrong at home. Things that if he were here would be of no consequence because we would rely on him to deal with these issues. Nothing life threatening I admit, but definitely stuff that always makes me think 'FFS why the hell are you away, drunk and living it up in a hovel somewhere and I'm left scrabbling around desperately trying to find my initiative in order to survive.' A few examples of the hiccups we have previously experienced are;

1. The large oak electric gates on our driveway breaking down and subsequently trapping us inside our own boundaries. Making it impossible to leave by car or on foot. Requiring a manual key to unlock, relock and turn the power off and back on again for each side of the gate separately. It is a task that would have taken Husband approximately 5 minutes but that took me over an hour in actual time and left me wondering if I had broken one of the locks and its associated key, which looked more bent than before I started. The worry of thinking I'd broken the fucking thing was actually worse than being trapped. Obviously it wouldn't have been worse if we had needed to let in the emergency services or had wanted to escape from zombies at short notice. That would have been a real problem. This happened two years running during his annual trip.

2. The gates opening and then downing tools and refusing to move or operate with any kind of power. Leaving us open to intruders, weirdos, doggers, deviants and zombies etc etc.
As I write this I am suddenly very aware that our gates are fucking shit and a large proportion of my life troubles seem to be connected to them.

3. A power cut which couldn't decide if it wanted to come back on or not, subsequently each time the power went off and then came back on, it triggered the burglar alarm to keep going off and scaring the shit out of us all.

4. A water cut. *I shit you not.* We were without water for a few hours and had a whole day with such low water pressure that it was impossible to flush the toilet, shower or use the washing machine and dishwasher.

5. Our house becoming the new nesting site for bats.

The time with the bat was the time Husband was in Silverstone for 4 nights. We'd somehow managed to make it 2 nights into his trip with no problems or occurrences. It put me on edge because I knew it was only a matter of time before something dreadful or frightening would happen that I would have no other option than to deal with in Husbands absence.

Settling down to a night of TV, the Anklebiters and I were snuggled up all cosy on mine and Husbands big bed in our room. It was warm and we had the french doors open that lead out to a small bedroom balcony as we did most evenings. Husband was forever warning against having these doors open, always trying to frighten me with stories of wildlife sneaking in when no one was looking. Obviously I never took any notice because it is in my job description as 'wife' that I usually ignore all his advice at all times. It was getting on for 10pm but it was the six week school holidays so there was no rush to get anyone to bed. The house needed one last nighttime check to make sure all doors were locked and windows closed before I could retire for the day.

Making my way downstairs I locked the front door, and was on my way to the kitchen to close windows and get some snacks for bed. On opening the kitchen door my head was nearly taken clean off my shoulders by a giant black pterodactyl!

Holy Fuck!

My stomach dropped clean out of my arshole. What the actual fuck was that? Acting on instinct alone I slithered to the floor and army crawled back out the way I'd come in, shutting the door after me. For what seemed like forever I sat there sweating and swearing and generally panicking as to what the absolute fucking hell that creature was flying around my kitchen.

We have a bit of an unconventional house layout whereby our ensuite bathroom overlooks the kitchen. Currently we have no window between the ensuite and kitchen, just a huge gaping hole where a window will eventually go once we pull our fingers out. It then dawned on me that if the pterodactyl was flying round the kitchen like it owned the place it was likely that it had flown through the windowless window, into the ensuite, into our bedroom and if our bedroom door was open, that would definitely be its ticket to free reign of the entire house.

I felt sick.

Tear arsing up the stairs shouting my head off, alerting the Anklebiters to the invasion and encouraging them to vacate the bedroom at lightning speed, it was clear I was scaring the crap out of them. Once they were out of the bedroom and on the safety of the landing I did the only thing I could think of to protect my babies and solve this issue.

I rang Mum.

'Mum, you need to come straight away, there's an enormous creature flying around the kitchen and I don't know how I'm going to catch it? Bring Step Dad and some creature catching tools.' I rambled breathlessly.
    'A creature? What sort of a creature?' Enquired Mum.
    'I don't know. Could be a pterodactyl, or a crow. I'm not sure which but it's definitely one of them.' I explained calmly, and in a whisper, like it could hear me.

Ten minutes later Mum and Step Dad turned up. Mum in her PJs and Step Dad brandishing a small blue fishing net suitable for catching goldfish but certainly not a pterodactyl. Seriously, what in God's name was he planning on doing with that?

Once inside the wildlife centre that was once our house we got our heads together and devised a cunning plan. It was decided that we would open the french doors at the back of the kitchen and turn on the outside lights. We would turn off the rest of the lights everywhere else in the house and keep all internal doors shut, encouraging the crow, that actually turned out to be a bat, to fly towards the light and out to freedom. To keep a very close eye on our little bat friend we paired up and I issued everyone a post. Step Dad and the smallest Anklebiter took the bedroom. Sitting in the dark they were under strict instructions to monitor and report any bat-related movements. Mum and the eldest Anklebiter were to stand in the kitchen near the open door so they could monitor if and when it left. This was an important post, perhaps the most crucial. Vital in the fight to prevent the nesting, breeding and starting of a new bat colony in the kitchen. I was left to nervously wander the rest of the house, hoping to God it hadn't managed to get loose and breach any other rooms.

Then came the shout from Stepdad. 'It's in the ensuite and heading your way!' Closely followed by this realisation the house was filled with high pitched frantic screams similar to those heard when riding the ghost train or the scariest roller coaster at the fair. Had the bat turned into a vampire? Had it picked up an Anklebiter and flown off with them? Had it attacked Mum and was now feasting on one of her limbs? Imagining all sorts of horrors I legged it downstairs into the kitchen where I was met with eerie silence. No movement at all. Proceeding with caution I searched the kitchen but there was no sign of anyone. Edging into the utility room now armed with the blue fishing net I was in full stealth mode. 'Mum?' I whispered tentatively. Suddenly the large doors to the boiler cupboard flew open and out tumbled Mum and eldest Anklebiter, unscathed it appeared, and giggling like they'd been at the laughing gas.

It turned out that no one had the faintest idea if the bat had left or not. It was explained later that when the bat had swooped from the ensuite window into the kitchen, instead of standing strong at their posts and defending our home with honour and bravery, they had abandoned their appointed positions and ran screaming into the cupboard where they had remained in silence waiting to be rescued.

For God Sake.

We reluctantly secured the house, unsure if our mission had been successful or not. The bat never surfaced again so it had either left while my soldiers were hiding in the cupboard or I expected to find it festering somewhere in a corner weeks later. Either way the flying and potential flesh eating vampire threat had subsided and the house was deemed safe again.

The bedroom balcony doors were not opened again for at least a week until I had forgotten the bat horrors that came before, and all normality resumed, ignoring Husband's advice once again and sleeping with them wide open during the warm nights. Thankfully that has been our only bat-related incident to date but you live and learn and I now know that if there was another of these incidents that I have 2 options.

1. Call on the shittest bat fighting team I know, aka- my family.
   Just for clarification I do mean 'shit' and not 'shit hot'

2. Do nothing. Let it nest and take over the house.

On reflection I have come to the conclusion it's quite likely both of these options would have exactly the same outcome and end with me running a bat sanctuary. **Harsh, but completely fair.**

The Worst Cafe Ever

Husband and I had made the executive decision to go out for tea. Loosely translated that meant he wouldn't be putting his chefs hat on anytime soon and I was sick to the back teeth of feeding the Anklebiters chicken nuggets every single night of their life except on the nights they had frozen smart price pizza. Because according to our 5 year old, the super cheap and nasty frozen pizza was the nicest one he'd ever eaten, obviously based on his extensive experience of italian cuisine.

 The trouble was I had created two tiny monsters where food was concerned. In the beginning my intentions had been good but it appeared I'd failed massively. But honestly if I were given my time again I'm not sure I'd do anything different because I did the best I could without starving them, being as mean as Hiltler and making the whole household's life a misery. As a toddler the eldest had eaten only the freshest, homemade purees. I had made a supreme effort to avoid jars and wanted to introduce healthy, tasty organic food. And for a minuscule snippet of her brand new life I had succeeded. It wasn't until she was older that she began to be difficult. Our second Anklebiter though had proved to be more tricky. When I started to wean him onto the same freshly pureed fruit and veg that I'd fed our first he would instantly throw up and then cry until I produced the baby food jars I was so against. The fruit and veg that had featured so strongly in the beginning was gradually replaced when the going got tough and the tantrums and refusal to eat kicked in. Don't misunderstand I didn't just one day say 'Fuck it I'm going to feed my kids nothing but nuggets until they're 18' and then threw out every last bit of remotely nourishing food. It was a lost battle here, and anything for an easy life there. I remember my brother being a fussy eater when we were kids and my mum worrying so much that he'd only eat banana on toast or cereal that she took him to the doctors to see what should be done. The doctor said there was nothing to be concerned about. He said not to worry because my brother wasn't underweight and it was probably just a phase that he would grow out of. Until then Mum was instructed to let him eat what he liked and not to pay too much attention, so at times with my little ones when it got particularly hard or I wanted to cry for being a bad mother, failing to raise my kids on organic everything, free from sugar and E numbers I thought back to the advice of the GP from the 80's. I reminded myself no one had died and calmly carried on.

So here we were a few years in, now living in a world of frozen nuggets, pizza, the occasional fish finger and at least 3 different types of oven chip because at least then I didn't have to look at the exact same type of chip day in and day out. Once in a while one of them might accidentally try something new, like when I pretended that a tempura prawn was an exotic strain of nugget or I bribed them to try lettuce, cucumber or garden peas in exchange for staying up late or a bag of haribos. Anyway this is the precise reason we thought tea out might be nice. The choices had been narrowed down to Ask or Prezzo. Italian was one of Husbands favourite foods and I could eat linguine as a profession, and until it came out of my nose. Final decision - Prezzo, because the food was lovely, and oh yes I nearly forgot

(of course I never pissing well forgot) they served pizza.

The car journey on route to the restaurant consisted of fighting, shouting and endless crying, mostly by our little 5 year old. Our eldest who was 7 and could talk you into oblivion without taking a breath was determined to keep him in line, true to her bossy nature and was desperately trying to calm him down by talking him to death, hence the fighting. As we pulled up into the car park I turned to look into the backseat. It had been eerily quiet for around 3 minutes but I hadn't dared look, frightened of what I might find. Had she thrown him out of the window? Suffocated him with the Peppa Pig travel pillow? Maybe she had shoved him under the driver's seat or pushed him through the trap door into the boot? What I actually found was the small one sleeping soundly and the bigger one lovingly stroking his hand like the loving little mother figure she was. My heart melted. Then it occurred to me we would have to wake him up to go into Prezzo and my very soul shrivelled up and ran screaming from my body. The transition from car to restaurant was suspiciously easy. It only made me wonder what he was saving up for when we were in the middle of the restaurant and in full view of the public eye.

The ordering process was quick and easy. I always had the same thing, prawn linguine. The kids ALWAYS had pizza and plain garlic bread and Husband ALWAYS chose something then wished he'd got something else when it arrived. After a rather speedy few minutes I could see the waiter approaching, garlic bread in hand, one with cheese but to my absolute horror the other had something on the top that resembled a tribe of dead slugs.

Oh shit.

I knew exactly how this would go down. The 5 year old was going to take one look at this sad excuse for a completely plain garlic bread and go fucking mental. When we had placed our order it had gone like this…

Me: Two margarita pizzas, a spicy prawn linguine and a ham and mushroom calzone please.

Waiter: Any starters today?

Me: Er, yes please. Two garlic bread, one with cheese and one plain.

Waiter: No problem Madam. *(Madam? Had I turned 80 years old and not noticed?)*

Me: Can I just make sure that the plain garlic bread just has garlic on it and nothing else.

Waiter: Yes of course.

Me: So just to be clear it won't have anything on top like cheese, or spicy tomato or caramelised onions or anything else you might feel like sprinkling on top?

Waiter: Not if you don't want anything on top.

Me: Or chilli pepper?

Waiter: You want chilli pepper?

Me: No definitely not. Just plain thank you.

Waiter *(Now looking a bit annoyed and confused):* Ok won't be long.

Now, clear as Husband's beard on his face the same waiter that promised me a completely plain garlic bread was now swaggering over here brandishing a fancy version without an ounce of shame. As the fancy garlic bread was put down in front of our 5 year old he just sat and stared at it. For what seemed like 3 years we all sat there holding our breath watching him watch his starter. He looked up at Husband and then back down at the food and then looked up at us again.

5yo: What is that?

Me: It's garlic bread for big boys.

5yo: I'm not a big boy, I'm 5.

Husband: It's got squashed up slugs on it, shall we boys try some *(trying to play the boy card)*

5yo: No thanks, I'm not eating any of it.

He said blowing his cheeks out and raising his eyebrows like an old man with anger issues. Following a bit of wheeling and dealing with another waiter who looked more superior, older and who I think was in charge of the whole operation we somehow by way of a miracle managed to get a plain garlic bread to the table before the 5 year old kicked off completely and all Holy Hell broke loose. Thank God. The main course was calm and went without incident, enjoyable even. We all thoroughly enjoyed the food and were discussing what we would be having for pudding. It was always going to be either chocolate cake or ice cream for the kids because they were their 'go to' desserts and a firm favourite whether at home or in a restaurant. Ice cream it was. When the waiter came back, pad in hand our little 7 year old ordered hers herself like she was a professional and had been doing it for years. She had always been advanced for her age and a real talker. She loved to chew the hind legs off a donkey, not interested whether she knew the person or not. Our 5 year old was much quieter. He had been a late starter speech wise and never really talked until he was 3 and then sounded a lot like he was from Easten Europe. So what a shocker it was when just as the waiter was leaving with our pudding orders that the little one piped up, 'Can I have strawberry sauce on mine please!!'

It had been an altogether very pleasant experience. I felt bad for feeling surprised but also grateful that we had managed to somehow escape any public humiliations in the form of tantrums, crying or fighting. Phew. The ice creams arrived. Both ankle biters dived in head first like it was the first time they'd been fed in a week when suddenly the 5year old stopped dead, spat his mouthful back into the bowl and pulled a most unattractive face, like he was doing a poo before screaming, 'What is that red stuff? I thought it was strawberry sauce. It's not strawberry sauce, it's horrible! THIS IS THE WORST CAFE I HAVE EVER BEEN IN !!!!'

And although he probably should have been reprimanded for his behaviour, we laughed. We really really laughed because it was comedy at its best coming out of an angry 5 year old's mouth and we loved it. Husband and I tend to laugh at inappropriate things and this was no exception. It turned out his complaint had been because the strawberry sauce was not the cheap sugar laden stuff he was expecting, it had been freshly prepared raspberry culee that is more appropriate to a nice eatery. So now years later, if we ever go anywhere to eat that's not as nice as we might have hoped we always say the same thing … 'This is the worst cafe we have ever been in!!'

Next to Rule the World is a French Icon

Primarily known as, and answers to, Sprout, The Hamster, Ferret Face, Small and The Coconutter, or on occasion her actual name which when used in full is Madam Coco Chanel. What other name could be more suitable for a French Bulldog other than the most French name, belonging to the most notorious French Icon who epitomises everything French? To avoid any confusion this is a story about Coco Chanel the Frenchie, not Coco Chanel the Fashion Designer. I have never referred to the latter as a Ferret Face.

Her story began when she arrived at our door unannounced early one Sunday morning accompanied by Husband's longtime good friend, The Gentle Giant. The Gentle Giant is a man that stands around 6ft 3, has a sprinkling of tattoos and a beard. He is built like a brick shit house and is the type who if you were to stumble across him down a dark alley would make you crap your pants on sight. At this point you would also question which prison he had escaped from. A horribly unfair assumption as he is actually the loveliest man we know with a heart of gold.

It was an ungodly hour for a Sunday. Certainly no later than 8am and I was in a lovely dream involving Jason Mamoa who was in mid-flow, proclaiming undying love for me. Imagine how annoyed I was at being rudely and inconsiderately torn from these thoughts by the sound of our house phone ringing and ringing and not stopping it would seem, ever. We have electric gates at the entrance to our driveway and this was an indication someone was at our gate requesting entry. The landline was never used for anything else since everyone including our eldest Anklebiter had a mobile phone. Last year we accepted that, at the age of 11, and on her way up to high school she was old enough for one. That and the fact that she'd chewed our ears off for months and months complaining she was the only one in her class at school that didn't own a phone. She also wanted to know what would happen if she got into a right pickle and had no way of contacting us. She made a compelling argument in the phone's favour. 'I have to catch the bus to school when I start secondary in September, what if I get beaten up by the older kids or get followed by a perv? How would I ring for help without a phone?' She had accused. She knew I was a sucker for a tale of abduction, perv related or otherwise. Some parents' deepest fears were about their kids choking, some about them being in a car accident or involved in bullying, mine was a kidnapping. The thought that among the legions of weirdos in the world that one of them might try and take my child when I wasn't there to protect them or when my back was turned for a minute made my blood run cold. Ever since both Anklebiters could walk I had always pushed the 'don't talk to strangers' rule, explaining that if they did they would almost certainly be stolen and would never see mummy and daddy again. This sounds like a harsh, scary thing to tell a toddler but I always thought it necessary to illustrate the importance of this rule. It was now being used as a tool against me in the acquisition of an iphone. And it worked.

Trying to ignore the shrill sound that was biting into my head and ruining my chances with Jason, I squeezed my eyes shut tightly, desperately trying to find my way back into the same dream but it was useless.

'Seriously? What's wrong with people? Who comes visiting at 8am on a Sunday?' I demanded loudly at Husband like he'd arranged it. As the words left my mouth I suddenly knew without a doubt who it would be. Hanging up the receiver, Husband confirmed my suspicions.

'It's Gentle Giant. I spoke to him yesterday and he mentioned he had a present for you. I didn't know he was dropping it in this morning though.' Said Husband looking surprised.
   'What sort of present?' I enquired, warming up slightly, but not much.
   'Not a clue. You know what he's like, it could be anything,' Husband replied.

As Gentle Giant exited his car he was greeted by our big American Bulldog, very fussy and enthusiastic, and brandishing a croc. In our house it is near impossible to cobble together a matching pair of shoes. This is down to our Bullys love for them. A croc, a trainer, an Ugg boot, a high heel, a sandal or God forbid, eldest Anklebiters Dr marten or Van, he doesn't discriminate. It's not that he chews or dismembers them, he just likes to carry them around and give them to visitors (or burglars) as gifts, which is totally fine but he gets distracted sometimes and leaves them in random places like the garden and the nearby foresty bit at the back of our house. A totally shit situation when I'm trying to find some shoes in a hurry and am faced with 6 separate shoes, none of which form a matching pair and I have to decide out of an Ugg and a sandal or a high heel and a trainer, which is the least offensive match to be seen on the school run in.

We greeted our visitor before I went back inside to make the drinks. Husband and Gentle Giant always sat on the porch, or in the garage. They very rarely came inside the house even in the depths of winter. It must be a man thing as I know I've never kept any of my guests on the porch, even the ones I'm not overly keen on. From the kitchen I could hear through the window the noisy exchange of pleasantries before Gentle Giant launched into a rowdy account of what had gone down at work on the building site last week. *I made that sound a bit like a drug deal or a firearms transaction but it wasn't anything as sinister or exciting.* From what I could gather they were discussing a worm of a man that they both knew who owed Gentle Giant some money and had done for quite some time. ' ... so I said to him, you've got 2 choices. You can cough up that money you owe me or take yourself back off into that house to finish your job and do not set foot outside of it for the rest of the day or I'll fill you in,' explained Gentle Giant followed by a raucous laugh.

Were these men really nearly 50? It seemed hard to believe sometimes. Interrupting more jackanory I took out the steaming cups of tea.

'I've got something for you, follow me.' Said Gentle Giant, looking at me with a wide smile plastered across his face. He turned and walked over to his car. On opening the passenger door a small black and white ferret jumped out and proceeded to fuss around our feet and explore its new surroundings.

'Who's this?' I questioned, bending down to stroke the ferret, which on closer inspection turned out to be a very small, scrawny French Bulldog.

'This is your new lodger. I thought that old bully of yours was ready for another partner in crime.' He said.

10 years ago we rescued our bully and also a beautiful girl Mastiff /Rottie. From separate places and a few months apart, once they got to know each other they became best friends, and got into plenty of mischief together. We had trawled the preloved adverts when we came across a picture of a strapping Mastiff Rottweiler cross. We were at the time making a move to the country and wanted to feel protected so she was just what we were looking for. When we went to look at her we got the distinct impression that the owner just wanted to get rid of her and didn't seem too bothered to whom. Whatever questions we asked, were answered in a way that made it sound like she could be whatever we wanted her to be. I'm positive that if I'd said we were only interested in a dog that was part giraffe, the owner would have confirmed that in fact she was. We collected her a few days later and brought her home to meet the family. She was the first dog we ever owned. A few months later we decided that she might like a friend of the canine variety and began a new

preloved pet search which is when we discovered our handsome American Bulldog Mastiff cross. The place we collected him from was far from luxurious but his owner was kind to him. She explained she worked 2 jobs and didn't have the time or money to keep him as she had only given him a home on a temporary basis. This was due to him being rescued from a flat full of young lads that found it amusing to get drunk and then abuse him in the most awful ways. I didn't need to hear anymore. That sealed the deal. We took him with us that same day. The dogs spent every day together until last year, when after a short illness our girl left this world for another. Since then our Bully had been in a deep depression that he couldn't shake. Once a fun loving, boisterous bundle of energy he had become a shadow of his former self following his best friends' departure.

This little ferret could be just what he needed to drag him back into the land of the living and help him be happy again. The only problem I could see was that he had an obscure fascination with things that were small and furry and generally was inclined to excitedly chew their heads off. I'm not being dramatic, he quite literally chewed the heads off anything small and furry that he could catch, and he was fast. If you were a rabbit or a guinea pig or a small French Bulldog that looked like a ferret you were done for. I was trying hard, but I couldn't see a happy ending. This was one of the reasons we had decided against getting another dog in the first place. A dog of his own size he would get thoroughly wound up about and want to play with but because of his size and power this was a considerably scary thing to witness, and a small dog he would try and eat. If we all made sure we gave him more cuddles, more kisses, more treats, more walks surely he would come around eventually, or so we had thought, but at just over a year on his own he wasn't making any progress.

'Where did you get her?' I enquired, nodding at the little dog that was now standing at Husband's feet staring up at him eerily.

'I was on a job on that really rough estate and got talking to one of the neighbours, he wanted to show me his puppy farm. It was fucking discusting. So many dogs were crammed into cages in his house and back garden. The stink made me gag.' He said looking annoyed.

Because of the way The Gentle Giant looked he was always being befriended by undesirable scumbag sorts who attempted to include him in their world. To which he would go along with so far, usually to serve a purpose before dropping them. Sometimes literally. He continued, 'This little lady was heading for a place of no return, she'd been raped so many times by the bigger dogs when she was young, she ended up in pup and she had a prolapse. All her lady bits had to be taken away meaning she can't have puppies so she was no good to him.'

My heart was breaking. This scrawny little thing just needed a loving home, something she'd never yet experienced in her short life. Gentle Giant continued to explain how he had thrown £100 on the table in this house of horrors before picking up the little dog and leaving with her, without a backward glance or permission. To be fair he's not the sort of bloke you challenge or disagree with if you know what's good for you, especially not when you are a revolting cruel puppy farmer. He'd also reported what he'd seen to the authorities so with a bit of luck the whole operation would be shut down and the rest of the dogs rescued.

'What about him?' Husband said, looking through the kitchen window at our Bully who, after catching sight of the little dog, was now steaming around the kitchen like a Motherfucker.

'I'll leave her for a few days and see if they get on, if they don't I'll come back for her and find her somewhere else,' said The Giant brightly, climbing back into his car. After a minute or two he was gone and all that remained was a tiny black and white ferret, Husband and me, all looking at each other not sure what to do next.

For the rest of that day we kept the dogs separate except for when they were under the strictest of supervision, always making sure Husband and I were both there in case a scuffle broke out and the ferret had to be rescued from the jaws of certain death. I hadn't seen our Bully so lively in months, admittedly it wasn't 'excited at having a new friend lively' but more, 'excited at having new prey to hunt lively', in fact it was plain to see when he stared at her he was seeing her as a giant pork chop or gammon joint with legs, just as Tom does in my favourite cartoon when he's imagining eating Jerry for lunch. By mid afternoon there had been a few close encounters which we had refereed extremely well, and managed to avoid any fatalities, so I decided to leave Husband in charge while I popped to the pet shop to get a few essentials. A cosy bed, a food bowl, a collar, dog shampoo, a teddy to stop her being scared during the night (probably when she would be dreaming about her own brutal demise at the hands of the savage monster in the next room that kept head butting the door to try and get in and finish her off.) She settled in better than expected. The following morning we came downstairs to find her snuggled in her new bed, a huge change from the cage she was used to, and only a small wee on the tiles. Could have been much worse.

I called the vet and got her booked in for that same morning. Just a once over to confirm she looked okay and wasn't going to peg it within the week. The Anklebiters had grown very fond of her in the whole 24 hours they had spent with her. Thankfully she got a clean bill of health. There were only a couple of issues that needed attention. She was underweight by quite a lot, and that was the reason she looked more like a ferret than the teeny tiny bulldog she was. We needed to feed her up to get her to the recognisable shape of a bulldog but that shouldn't be a problem because she was a greedy little thing. The other problem was a big problem for me.

She had fleas.

And apparently not just a few floating around but 'riddled with them' as quoted by the vet following a dramatic and possibly unnecessary gasp. Had it been me that made this gruesome discovery then there would have been a shit load of gasping and swearing, and also crying, but she was supposed to be an animal healthcare professional and in my opinion should be used to such grisly discoveries. How I hadn't noticed I just don't know. All I could think about was my house would now be crawling with them, making nests and setting up home in my cushions and throws for the foreseeable future. The brand new cosy little bed I'd purchased only the day before would now be good for nothing except to light a bonfire with. I voiced my concerns to the vet and was steered in the direction of the industrial strength flea spray that apparently saves pet owners from having to burn down their houses and all their possessions because of a few fleas. One treatment would kill everything and one can did 2-3 treatments. That was the promise on the label anyway so just to be sure I bought 3 cans. I wasn't taking any chances, I planned to do a few applications. Within a week I had used 2 lots of the spray but kept the third on ice, waiting in the wings for the day a ballsy flea army dared to attempt re-entry back into our lives. When they did I'd be ready to wipe them off the face of the planet. Maybe not the planet but definitely out of our home.

Strangely after a couple of days of incessantly trying to kill this peculiar little dog, our Bully just gave up the desire to do her in and without warning, approved of her all of a sudden. As quickly as he would have in the past, ripped her head off, he just stopped. It was like he realised out of nowhere that she was staying and would be joining our family for good and that he should accept his fate quietly. So that's what happened. In fact they began to get along marvellously. Play fighting and chasing each other, it was lovely to see. None of us had seen our Bully behave this way since his old pal left, and this new little dog seemed like she was having the time of her life. As we got to know her better we realised what a big character she was despite her little body. We found out she was sassy and surprisingly not frightened of anything. It's a regular occurrence that she will offload her faecal matter right in the middle of the kitchen floor whilst looking right at us, despite having just come back from an hour long walk. I'm certain it's deliberate to make sure we know our place, which she believes is below her in the pecking order, putting her in charge.

The fleas were gone, the children were in love and Husband was utterly captivated with our new little dog. Our bully hadn't tried to kill her lately and it had been nearly 2 weeks so it was settled that she would stay.

There's something about small dogs that makes you believe they are innocent and can in no way be to blame for anything, even when you catch them in the act of whatever bad behaviour they are showcasing. Maybe it's because they're little and cute, I'm not sure, but what I do know is that Husband has fallen head first into this trap. I frequently catch him speaking to her in a baby voice, the same as you might speak to a toddler. Even when her behaviour is horrendous, chewing shoes, and breaking into the best living room to poo all over the cream carpet, after an initial outburst he seems to get over it in record time, reiterating to me how it's not her fault. Sometimes he tags at the end of this statement 'She's just a baby.' I have to explain that at the age of 2 (so the vet thinks), she isn't a baby, she's fully aware of how naughty she is and how I can almost hear her doing a wicked laugh knowing full well she has tricked Husband and has got him right where she wants him.

6 months into our new role as small dog owners and there have been a few hair raising moments. Not usually the type of family to panic, there have been at least 2 occasions when we thought she might die. Once after a mad half hour charging around in the garden she was so puffed out that she started having what looked like a seizure but made a suspiciously speedy recovery just as I was about to call the vet. The other time she had diarrhoea and sickness so badly, my entrance hall looked like shit had been sprayed liberally out of a hosepipe all over the entire floor, both dog beds and part of the wall. Small piles of

sick also littered the poo-filled room. I had returned home to find this mess with her laid amongst it, shaking terribly. Again, I duly noted that once she had been bathed and the entrance hall had been dealt with, that the shakes stopped at the speed of light and she could be found sniffing around the biscuit cupboard.

It's been puzzling me but I have come to realise what is happening.

Not only does she wrap Husband around her little paw, tricks us into thinking she is about to die so we all run around after her and treat her like the Queen of Sheba but I have noticed lately that she is now the boss of our Bully. He is her minion and she controls his every move. She has him knock down the stair gate we have at the bottom of the stairs so she can run up to our bedroom and leave us a turd beside our bed. Our bullys' other talent apart from losing approximately 27 shoes a month is that he can open doors. Freakish and rather annoying at times but she now gets him to open the living room door. The place they are forbidden to go to because of the cream carpet and the silly idea that we might try to keep at least one room 'for best'. On entry she empties her bladder all over the settee and then runs around shitting at will all over the carpet. This has happened more than once.

I think I may have discovered what she is up to. I predict that it will only be a matter of time before she takes over completely and will soon be running our whole house. She will knock Husband off his throne as head of the family and take her rightful place. From here the world will be her oyster and with her main Bully minion to assist her, she will systematically put a cunning plan in place to set the wheels in motion for world domination.

Pirate Dreams

Last Saturday, totally by accident I nearly achieved my lifelong ambition of becoming a pirate.
'Why a pirate?' I hear you whisper. Well who wouldn't want to be a pirate? That's a better question. With so many great things about being a villain of the sea where do I begin?

- A supercool occupation. Can we call it an occupation? Or is it more of a hobby? I'm just trying to picture in my head where it would look least suspect on an application form. Imagine getting into a conversation with someone and getting onto the topic of how you earn a crust. They tell you they are a nurse and in turn you casually drop it into the chat that you are in fact, a pirate. WOW. Your street cred is now through the roof.

- Bandannas and hoop earrings. Both firm favourites of mine. When I wear a headscarf it is mainly because my hair is dirty and smelly and hasn't seen a shower or a sniff of dry shampoo in weeks. **Yes, weeks.** I can only assume this is the same for a pirate. When you are busy hunting for treasure and capturing innocent people to walk the plank, I suspect the last thing on your mind is giving your hair a thorough deep conditioning treatment.

- Drink loads of rum. Self explanatory. Also I may have to modify this slightly into a rum based mojito. Small change. Hardly noticeable.

- Impressive language. They say stuff like 'Shiver me timbers, there's been a mutiny.'

- Eye patches. They get to make the biggest fashion statement this side of Milan by sporting a very edgy eye patch. Think Gabrielle, think Madonna. Not so much the strange chap from Harry Potter with the funny protruding eye.

- Parrots. A pet that you can teach rude words to and possibly even converse with. I bet the cleverer ones can use guns and learn how to sword fight which is singularly the best thing ever - to have a sword fighting, gun wielding parrot, except, probably not in everyday life like at the supermarket because that would be weird and I bet Asda wouldn't be overly keen on it, but you know what I mean.

To further support my love of pirates let me draw your attention to the text message exchange I had with my friend a few months back.

Me: I was stung by a wasp yesterday. Might have to have my leg off. Just wanted to brief you in case I only have one leg next time you see me.

Patricia: Oh no, are you okay? Are you having it off above or below the knee? I recall you also mentioning an eye patch quite a lot just lately. One leg and an eye patch, you'll do anything to be a pirate won't you.

My Pirate dream is clearly no secret but the last thing I expected was that it might happen for real, or at least part of it.

Walking our dogs through the fields around our house is a favourite weekend pastime that the whole family takes part in. Some are more willing participants than others. Okay, the Anklebiters actually hate it and we have to threaten them to make them come along but Husband and I enjoy it. This particular Saturday however, Husband was busy dismantling one of his motorbikes and when I set off on the walk he was sitting in the garage chin deep in 100,000 parts and wearing an upside down smile. The second the kids had got a sniff of a dog walk they had legged it and hidden so it was just the dogs and me. We went our usual route but it had been raining and the ground was a thick muddy mess. It was a real task to keep to the edge of the field off the crops because the verge was so slippery. The wind was battering my face and it had just started to rain again making it tricky to see. This wasn't going to be one of the most enjoyable walks but rather than bitch about it and chunter to myself the whole 3 miles round I put my shoulders back, mustered some enthusiasm, held my head high, and promptly walked into a rogue branch face first and got speared through my left eyeball.

Holy Fuck that hurt.

Instantly my hand flew up to my face to cover the damaged area. After standing there for what seemed like an eternity I reluctantly moved my hand. Was my eye still in my socket or hooked on the branch? I couldn't tell but I definitely had a bit of twig stuck behind my eyelid. It felt weird and if I tried to open it I knew for certain my eyeball would fall out, if it was actually still in there at all. Panic swept over me. After all, this was my eye, this was serious shit. Suddenly I had visions of me looking demure in an eye patch. Good God maybe this really was my destiny, to become a famous pirate. Or just a pirate. Or just someone who was forced to wear an eye patch due to a freak branch accident but wasn't cool enough to be a pirate. Who knew? Battling on, we made it the whole way round. I'd managed by some miracle not to cry and also not to gouge out the other eye. Cold, soggy and half blind I limped down the driveway to be greeted with Husband leaving the garage and asking me why I was winking at him. After explaining what had happened and voicing my concerns about losing my eye for good, mentioning the bit of twig that was definitely under my eyelid, Husband did exactly what I knew he would do.

Show concern, play nurse and look after me?

NO.

Bundle me into the car without any regard for his afternoon plans and rush me to the hospital or the eye clinic?

NO.

Call an ambulance, explaining it was a life and death situation because his beautiful wife may lose an eye and then may have no choice but to become a pirate.

You've probably guessed, also NO.

What he did do, was absolutely nothing. Except over the course of the afternoon kept periodically asking me if I was winking at him again.

Taking matters into my own hands I bathed my eye in warm water, trying to swish out the stick that was trapped in there but it wasn't budging. After drying off my face I realised it felt more comfortable when my eye was closed so I taped my eyelid shut. Trying to negotiate your way around anywhere, even your own home with just one eye is a nightmare. I didn't realise how much you actually need both eyes to keep your balance. With this in mind I feel I've made some inaccurate assumptions about pirates and may need to review my opinion. I always assumed they were staggering around drunk from all the rum they had consumed, when in fact I now believe it's definitely a side effect of wearing an eye patch and only having the use of one eye. This revelation has made the pirate proposition less attractive now as I realise that I won't be continually drunk but just a bit blind. I may have to rethink the whole thing.

That afternoon we watched a film as a family in the big living room with the log burner roaring. It was lovely. I didn't see a great deal of the film, because you don't see much with one eye, but I enjoyed the family time. The youngest Anklebiter had been in charge of film choice and had gone with one starring 'The Rock' who would save the world against a giant gorilla and a man eating crocodile that was bigger and meaner than Godzilla. It ended with 'The Rock' asking the giant gorilla for help killing the Psycho crocodile because it turned out that the gorilla was his friend and they used sign language to communicate before the accident that had mutated him into a monster. The scene that finished off the film saw the gorilla kill the crocodile by spearing him through the eye with an enormous sharp object.

'Right through the eye into his brain.' Shouted our youngest with sheer delight. It was like I was watching a reenactment of what had happened to me that afternoon but unlike the crocodile I had survived. I'd been closer to death's door than I thought, just a couple of millimetres further in and who knows what would have happened?

I still think pirates are bloody brilliant but I have reassessed my stance on actually becoming one. I'm not promising I won't turn up on a night out or to someone's wedding wearing a magnificent diamond encrusted eye patch, but for now I won't be making it my full time job.

Luckily after a dodgy few days my eye felt much better and thankfully to date it hasn't fallen out or rolled back to front or anything freaky like that so that's a bonus.

The House that Husband Built, not Jack

It had always been an ambition of Husbands to build his own house. So 10 years ago that's what happened.

At 6 months pregnant with our second Anklebiter, selling our beautiful little Victorian end terrace was a stretch for me. Engulfed with all the memories from raising our first born there, it was emotional to say the least. I was a hormonal disaster zone and on top of that making sure the house was immaculate at all times for the crowds of time wasters that came to view, week in week out was difficult.
Hearing choruses of 'Oh it's lovely, just what we're looking for, if only it had 2 extra bedrooms and a garage,' was unbelievable to me. What was wrong with people? When a house is advertised on Rightmove or other respective selling sites you'd think the general public might actually take notice of the valuable information on offer before booking a viewing, like how many bedrooms they need and how

many the house they choose to view (sometimes twice or more) has, before realising that their family wont fit in it. Inconsiderate morons. It felt like certain families were deliberately seeing how many times they could make me clean it, lugging my baby bulk around, breathless and sweating before the lightning strike moment hit them that our house had 3 bedrooms but they really wanted 5 to accommodate their 8 children. The truth of the matter was they couldn't afford what they wanted so would reserve a Sunday afternoon for a lovely day out, relentlessly snooping around someone's house just for an outing.

Early one Sunday morning in particular a few months later, we had a surprise knock at the door. On answering we found 2 people we'd never laid eyes on before who announced that they had seen our house and thought they would come for a look. Really? Absolutely. Don't bother calling the agent and booking an appointment like normal well balanced Humans, just rock up at 8.30 unannounced on a Sunday morning and ask to view a complete stranger's house. Totally acceptable. **I think not.** Still horribly hormonal but now with a very small baby, a rational thought had not entered my head for weeks. After a quick eye discussion with Husband at the door (looking at each other and knowing what we were thinking without the use for words) while they stood on our step awkwardly, it was decided that on this occasion we would overlook the lack of appointment and asked them to give us a couple of hours and come back at a more reasonable time later in the day. After all, they could potentially be our buyers. Lunchtime came and went and when they hadn't returned I was relieved. These people could be anyone. We didn't know them from Jefferey. Settling in to the idea that we had dodged a bullet and avoided a potential gunpoint robbery or murder (the woman was wearing an overly large coat and could have easily had a concealed weapon,) we went about our business for the day. Just about to dish up the roast that had taken me the best part of the day to do, between nappy changes and feeds there was another knock at the door.

Fuck off. It couldn't be?

Well it was. Not only had they had the audacity to return over 8 hours later but a few minutes into the viewing it became fairly obvious they were leathered. Reeking of drink, they weaved their way around our house. Upstairs, Husband had just shown them the recently completed shower room. 'Oh I like this room, it's great.' Slurred the drunk man to his drunk wife. As Husband led them out of the shower room and was about to take them back downstairs and out of our lives, the man spun round to the door they had just come from and said, 'What's in here?' It really was time for them to go now. Before Husband could lose his shit and possibly use the drunk woman's own concealed weapon on her, I escorted them out and locked the door.

All in all the viewings and odd bods came and went for a few months. Once we had eventually sold, the estate agent told us that we'd had the most online views recorded and at an average of 4 viewings per week over the last 5 months our property had been the most popular on their books. We had accepted offers twice previously before actually closing the deal the lucky third time around.

Rewind 3 months. Back to when I was mostly showing around time wasters everyday of my massive pregnant life.

Also at the time of mercilessly dragging people around our house day and night we had seen a piece of land for sale. It was on a small plot, in a village an hour away from our current location and would have suited us down to the ground. In order to proceed with buying anything before we had successfully sold our own we had remortgaged ourselves into the depths of Hell so that we were in a good position should any opportunities arise. Unfortunately after attempting to buy this land 3 times it became apparent that the agent selling it had another agenda. Each time our offer was accepted a week later the vendor would apparently change their mind, pull out and then the process would begin again. After the third sale fell through, our nerves couldn't take any more and we decided to look for pastures new. I don't believe in chance or coincidence. I wholeheartedly subscribe to the theory that everything happens for a reason and if something that was planned doesn't come off in the way you wanted, it's because it wasn't meant to be and something else is.

How right I was.

One night Husband was in the bath reading the paper. In the days before everyone owned an ipad, laptop or smartphone and it was the norm to take to a bubble bath reading what would become a slightly flaccid soggy newspaper. He called me in to show me the postage stamp sized advert he had accidentally stumbled across on the second to back page.

Cast your mind back.

No one ever read the very back pages unless you were scanning the free ads or were a MBA male HNG seeking BBW with GSOH for F2FRL meetings. To those not privy we have just unearthed a MARRIED BUT AVAILABLE male HORNY NET GEEK seeking a BIG BEAUTIFUL WOMAN with a GOOD SENSE OF HUMOUR for FACE TO FACE REAL LIFE meetings. Seriously it's no wonder these people never met anyone. Anyway, regardless of what Husband might have been doing amongst these suspicious offerings, the advert he showed me would be the start of our dream.

A white washed, broken down, derelict cottage dating back to the 1800s looked back at me from the paper. In the same neck of the woods as all my family and only a 20 minute drive from Husband's, it was perfect. It would be sold by sealed bids in a week's time.

Sealed bids. A process that invites you to write down an amount of money you are willing to pay for the property in question with no idea how much anyone else will be offering. There is usually a guide price and the sale usually falls in favour of those with the highest bid and/or in the best position. Maybe those who do not need a mortgage because they have cash in the bank or those not in a chain.

After calling to book a viewing I was told that if I could make an 8am appointment the following day then I could view. I would be the first of 22 viewings that day and it was the only space left. Wow. At least 22 parties interested. It would be a battle, but one I was ready for. I'd only seen the small smudgy picture but already I felt it was meant for us. Husband couldn't get off work so all responsibility of looking around the property, accessing the work needed and asking the relevant questions fell to me.

Oh dear.

Not great at things that require logical thinking and rationale, I could already see how this might unfold. More of a, if the feelings right get it, sort of a person I was probably the least qualified to undertake a task such as this. It was also the only viewing day before the deadline when all bids would be opened so Husband wouldn't be able to look round it at all. It really was all down to me to make some good decisions. A very dangerous game to play.

The day was cold and I had opted for a wool poncho type affair to keep out the wind. Now at 8 months pregnant I looked more like the side of a bus than I'd hoped for. Never one of those pregnants who was mistaken for not being pregnant and just having eaten a good meal, both my pregnancies made people question if I was in training to audition for a job as a fat-a-gram.

Looking around the derelict building I could smell the damp and the rotten wood unique only to unoccupied unloved spaces often frequented by smack heads. *I imagine.* It was in a terrible state, there were no two ways about it. Crumbling walls, smashed windows, gaps in the roof where I assume tiles had once been, and not a kitchen in site. Some very questionable decor, one of the rooms was fuchsia pink in colour with black playboy rabbit stencils all over the walls. Most likely to have been a child's room at some point in its life, it could also easily have been a porn dungeon. Definitely one or the other. The only appropriate course of action would be to bulldoze the cottage. As lovely as it could be with work, the sheer magnitude of this was unimaginable. Take the cottage out of the equation for a moment and you were left with the most wonderful setting. Set back from the road by a long straight driveway of at least 200 metres which was overhung with trees, it had a field at each side and a vast overgrown copse to the back making it a private piece of paradise. I loved it. Knowing full well I had found out nothing and asked a total of zero relevant questions, I thanked the agent, left and rang Husband immediately.

'What was it like?' He asked, without pleasantries.

'I love it, it's wonderful,' I said honestly. 'What about the work? How bad is it?' He questioned.

'Not bad really,' I heard myself say. 'The downstairs needs a bit of fixing up but the upstairs wasn't so bad. Nothing you can't handle'; A bear faced lie. Could he feel the heat of my face through the phone?

The next day we made an unscheduled visit for an unsolicited nosy parker. The bids were due in by the end of the day so it gave Husband a chance to at least experience the unrivalled setting without actually seeing all of the work involved. Having no key there's only so much that can be seen from outside, or from looking through broken windows into a porn dungeon. Husband seemed as happy as me. We had agreed a price that was maybe slightly over the odds, given the state of it but I couldn't bear the thought that we wouldn't get it and someone else would move into my dream place. The next few days were tense. These things take time and no one rushes to make a decision. Every time the phone rang I had to scrape myself off the ceiling. How I didn't give birth in those few days I don't know. Then came the phone call. The one we'd been expecting with the news we could have only hoped for.

It was ours. The games had begun.

When we discuss the purchase now, we look back with fondness about how I told Husband it needed a paint job when what I really meant was full demolition. Something that at the time, and on first inspection after receiving the keys left Husband speechless and looking a bit like he wanted to cry.

The weekend after it was made official, we took a little road trip to visit our new place to look around and generally be smug about it. Driving down the long driveway we noticed there were two people behind the hedge in one of the fields next to the cottage. A few minutes passed and no one surfaced so Husband went to investigate. In no time at all he reappeared red faced and chuntering something about perverts.

What? Perverts? What?

It turned out he'd walked in on 2 men going at it like rabbits ... in the middle of a field ... on a Saturday morning. It later came to our attention that the layby on the main road next to our driveway entrance was a notorious dogging spot, frequented mostly by blokes looking for a bit of chap on chap action. Not always just blokes though. A couple of years later, in the same layby, we accidentally saw a woman dressed in nothing but a suit jacket and a pair of high heels giving a blow job to a bloke like she hadn't eaten in months. 'By accident', I mean we both had binoculars and a cup of tea. That was also on a Saturday morning. Day time public sex sessions seemed to be all the rage. Don't misunderstand, we weren't perving on the pervs. It's just important, we thought, to take an interest in the local area. This became a new game for Husband. Although I know he hated what was happening, there was no mistaking his satisfaction when he recognised the same cars arriving and leaving the layby. He would stand on the top scaffold that surrounded the cottage and shout abuse at them, making sure they knew his view that they were weirdos who should piss off out of his layby. It was not his layby, he didn't own it, but being situated by our house he thought gave him the authority to try and police what was going on in there. Understandably no one wants an orgy going on in their front garden, or very close to it. On occasion if the offending deviants had the balls to shout back or not get in their vehicles and leave immediately, he would chase them in his car, on his motorbike and now and again on foot. I enjoyed his pursuits on foot the most. He had a huge ginger beard at this point and was constantly covered in brick dust making his facial and head hair stand on end. Chasing vehicles in his flip flops or crocs he looked like the wildman of Borneo.

Following the successful purchase of our dream bombsite, the sale of our terrace came shortly after. Off the back of some careful consideration it was decided the only sensible option would be to live onsite so we could save money on rent and always be on hand to get the work done. We thoughtfully chose an old static caravan, and by thoughtfully I mean the only one that was in our budget and by we, I mean I chose it, as Husband was once again unavailable due to work commitments and had let me loose with the credit card to make more bad decisions. Will this man ever learn? Due to this we were the proud new owners of an ancient mobile home which was an 1980s original with leaky windows and air conditioned doorways.

Home sweet home.

This 2 bedroomed, 12 footer would be our home as it turned out for the next 2 years. Husband and I, a toddler, a baby, his older girls most weekends and 2 large dogs that we had acquired along the way, because it's unheard of to live in the sticks without any form of protection, and what better was there than 2 vicious guard dogs. When the caravan had been delivered the man in charge was one of these sorts that fancied himself. He thought that he was a bit of a wide boy and that nothing could ruffle his feathers, until I introduced him to one of our dogs. She was the loyalist, most gentle dog I've ever had the honour of owning. Very protective of our family, especially the children she was never very keen when anyone unknown to her got too close. She also didn't like men. Whether she maybe had a run in with a man at one time or another before she came to us I don't know, but I do know she wasn't in the habit of entertaining them. When he had shown up in the morning to deliver the caravan, all loud and brassy I knew she would be a handful for me. She was on her lead so I could maintain some level of control but she was a big strong dog. He admired her and commented on what a beautiful dog she was.

It seemed her growling and show of teeth did nothing to discourage his enthusiasm. Being the good sport that I am, I thought it only fair to warn Mr Brassy so I asked him to keep his distance explaining she didn't like men she didn't know.

'Dogs love me.' He flounced confidently. Completely ignoring me, he approached us, keen to get a stroke in despite my warning. I wasn't wrong about her size and strength. It didn't take much for her to pull her head through her collar and bound over to meet his gesture by jumping up, knocking him to the floor and pinning him there, her snarling face an inch away from his. He looked less cocky now, walking back to his car visibly shaken and covered in mud and footprints. Not a great addition to the shirt and tie he had on. Not when we were first drop off and he probably had to attend a few more deliveries that day looking the scraggy mess he now did. But dogs did love him so I'm sure it was fine.

Both our dogs were recue dogs and although obtained for guarding purposes there was only our beautiful girl that embraced her role. The other dog, the same one we still have today, our handsome American Bulldog X had a taste, not for intruders unfortunately but for the caravan furniture. The whole of the left side of the built in settee including the arm had been eaten one morning and had remained that way until I had tried to sell it back to Mr Brassy a couple of years later. I was offered a goodwill gesture of £200 and the advice that I should take the offer as it was only on the table because he turned out to be my friend's new stepdad and what he'd really like to do is show it a box of matches. Harsh I thought and a bit rude. If truth be told I reckon he was still sore about the 'dogs love me' incident. It transpired I was right on the money when the month afterwards we had driven past the caravan place only to see our lovely home there at the front with a price tag for nearly as much as we had paid for it 2 years previously. **Robbing dog loving bastard.**

It appeared that caravan living agreed with us. Not a fan of housework, especially after all the cleaning up I'd undertaken in the last year to sell our terrace, I was ecstatic to learn that a full thorough deep clean took 20 minutes. It wasn't just the cleaning aspect I loved. Everyday felt like an adventure, like we were really living life. Daring to reside in a caravan on a building site with 2 kids, 2 dogs, no running water and no oven we were balancing precariously on the cusp of civilised existence. We were living like there was no tomorrow and on a more serious note that was a strong possibility. We were at times, I believe fairly close to catching cholera and in turn dicing with subsequent death. With no running water, we relied on filling 10 litre containers with tap water from Mums and Aunties. This would allow us to make drinks and wash up after being boiled using the kettle. Sometimes if Husband couldn't be bothered to go to Mums or Aunties for a shower following a particularly gruelling day he'd fill a small rhino tub usually used for builders cement, and get washed down in 3 inches of water before falling into bed exhausted. Because it was all so far from the mundane we all relished it, even welcomed it. Sometimes I could go a week without a proper shower. Eeking it out with a few half hearted wet wipe washes in between. Basically gross, but it happened. When the Anklebiters were a bit older and I had the school run to contend with I would wear my 10 year old battered split Hunter wellies because literally everything on a building site is mud mud and more mud, a cap to cover 2 week greasy hair and red lipstick to draw the attention away from all the aforementioned. Afterwards I would learn from another parent that I had been labelled 'glamorous' by the other mums on the playground because of this. It fascinated but didn't surprise me that people were so very quick to form opinions about me purely based on some wellies, a cap and some red lippy. Clearly they'd never had the bad luck to stand down wind from me when I was due a wet wipe wash. I'm certain I didn't smell glamorous.

Husband still refers to those times in the caravan as the best of his life. He truly loved being a smelly old gypsy.

This part might be boring so skip it if you like but you'll miss how we became personal friends of Her Majesty Queen Liz. Okay, not personal, or friends actually but a distant acquaintance (loosely). The cottage had originally been part of the Crown Estate which basically means it was owned by the Queen. When we signed all the paperwork for the purchase at the solicitors, the transfer document had the details of buyer and seller on the front. We were named as buyers and the seller was named as HRH. No lie! What we didn't realise at the time was that all proceeds from Crown Estate sales go to the chancellor and because of this they wanted to squeeze as much extra cash out of us as possible. Demanding we seek approval for anything we wanted to do to the property even though we owned it. The excuse being that the surrounding land was still owned by HRH and that it had to be what they deemed as suitable. Probably so we didn't build anything mad like a big glass spaceship or similar, I understand that. But what we did find difficult to swallow was that they wanted to charge us fees for gaining their approval. Always on the make. Having initiated an architect and eventually obtaining all the relevant consents the house was underway. The finished article would be a 3 story, white washed, double fronted traditional looking farmhouse with black wooden cladding and bifold doors to the back. We had managed at last to negotiate a mortgage so we could start the work, not an easy thing to do when the property you want to mortgage is appraised as being uninhabitable. As luck would have it I knew someone who was a retired valuer. Following a conversation about the struggles of having a mortgage approved in our situation it was discovered that someone who he used to work with was now head valuer for the bank we were pursuing for our mortgage. After a sneaky phone call between my friend and the head valuer, we were told to build a makeshift kitchen and to make sure the cottage had a toilet, working or not. Husband got his hands on an old sink and tap and fixed it to a couple of breeze blocks in the kitchen area. The toilet, although not working, still had the appearance of a toilet. So when the valuer turned up, although not a luxury set up, he passed it and the mortgage was in the bag. We knew it wouldn't be a quick project. It would have to be done bit by bit and after spending the initial funds on getting up the shell and doing a huge double extension to the side and replacing the roof the rest we would complete when we could afford it. But we had a plan and stuck to it.

It was during the replacement of the roof that Husband came unstuck one day. Quite literally. He lost his footing and fell from the top scaffold into a pile of rubble and old window frames peppered with rusty nails, narrowly escaping being speared through the head, he survived. Somewhat battered and bruised with a few corking scrapes it was a miracle really.

Our youngest Anklebiter was 3 at the time and wrote a story about it in the only way a 3 year old could, including pictures. This is still top of the list as one of my most favourite things.

Before the project of the main house began, Husband built a triple garage with a flat above. It was fully furnished and had a kitchen, living area, bathroom and bedroom. Once this was livable I sold our beloved old rickety caravan that I had grown to love, back to Mr Brassy for the rip off price of £200. We moved into the flat above the garage as soon as it was finished, which although was a step closer to humanity, was still essentially a garage. The eldest Anklebiter was around 4 at this time and took great pleasure in telling anyone that would listen, especially school teachers, that she lived in a garage. On a daily basis I fully expected social services to pay us a visit and with this in mind made a trip to school to explain our set up. That we didn't keep our children in the garage and that there was a fully functional flat above it where we would reside until the house build was finished. It was our home for a further 2 years and we had some of our happiest times there. Only having one bedroom, we crammed in a double bed and 2 singles for the Anklebiters. I loved the closeness of having my little family all together, safe in one room.

Now, we live in the actual house that Husband built, a beautiful 5 bedroomed dream. He did a marvellous job and although I probably don't say it enough, I'm very proud of him. It was a colossal vision we had and he made it happen. Still not completely finished I'm not sure it ever will be. There's always a project to undertake, jobs to do and things to fix but that's only like any other family home. Everyone now has their own rooms and their own space but the smallest Anklebiter still says he preferred our old house, meaning the garage. And I love that. Clearly we did something right, making memories when they were small. The majority of their early childhood was spent in pjs and wellies, no matter what the season and usually up a tree, on a 40 ton pile of gravel or driving a forklift with daddy. Hopefully it will be something they look back on as fondly as I do.

An Accomplice to Murder

Can you think of a better present for your 7th birthday than a pet rabbit? No? Neither could our eldest Anklebiter, and once she had her heart set on that one particular thing, that's all we heard about until we couldn't take it anymore and agreed to her terms. Once it had been decided for definite that we would welcome a small furry into the bosom of our family there were 2 fundamental issues that needed to be addressed.

1. Where would it live?

2. How would it get along with our old American Bully who, his whole life had swayed towards being obsessed with small furry creatures, and not in a good way.

Husband being the evil ebay genius that he was, managed to source a wonderful preloved 2 storey luxury rabbit hutch. It was top of the range, probably nicer than some people's houses and complete with a lounge, staircase and separate bedroom with ensuite. By ensuite I mean it had enough room for the small furry to sleep and comfortably poo its little head off all night long for a week without it becoming too cramped.

The second issue was going to be more difficult to solve. Our lovely American Bulldog X Mastiff had identity problems through no fault of his own. He simply looked differently to how he actually was. Similar to a heavily tattooed man with lots of piercings, a huge beard and a dirty mouth, clad head to foot in leather who likes to ballet dance and embroider in his spare time. People who didn't know our Bully looked twice because at first glance you could be forgiven for thinking he was a vicious brute of an animal. The truth is he is the gentlest, most loving, soft sappy dog anyone could ever hope to meet, except where small animals are concerned. He has always had an unhealthy infatuation with anything smaller than himself such as cats, guinea pigs, rats, mice, weasels, hares and rabbits, to name a few. We live in the country so he has been exposed to all of the aforementioned small furries in the past and on no occasion has it ended well. **Not for them**

anyway. A few years ago pre Anklebiters, when Husband's older girls were little we had been badgered to death about getting guinea pigs. After giving in we acquired 2 of them. They seemed to live forever until one of them eventually died, the other was invincible and refused to follow suit. At the equivalent age of around 167 in human years it still limped on and even survived a house move with us. It was only the acquisition of our Bully that saw its demise. Each morning when I'd let the dog out to do his business, the first thing he would do was sprint over to the guinea pig house and repeatedly head butt it. I assume his plan was to do this until the hutch collapsed and he could gain access. After the first time this happened, each morning I was ready for him and managed to deflect the outcome that was always going to happen. A few weeks into this new ritual and one morning as anticipated I wasn't quick enough. I looked on in horror as I saw him complete his mission, gaining entry and leaving with his prize, which he promptly chewed up a bit and left at the door of my car. Poor ancient guinea pig. For this reason, I predicted the planned new addition to our family would be stressful and fairly problematic. There would be no room for error and I would need to be on the ball at all times, supervising the shit out of them.

 One glorious morning in July the week of Anklebiters birthday we made a trip to our local pet shop to make some crucial pet picking decisions. The rabbit had to be just right. Not too big, not too hairy, not too jumpy, not too quiet, these were all important considerations that we had to be aware of when making the selection. What's the use in having a crazy lunatic bunny that no one could catch or hold? Or equally as annoying, one that just sat there, fat and bored and that needed to be poked with a stick to see any action. **Just for clarity, I have never poked any of our pets with a stick but not everyone is as humane as me and some, I'm sure partake in a spot of pet stick poking.** The one we came away with was neither of these things. He was small and cute, mainly white with a splattering of black patches. Most importantly he wasn't scared and seemed to like us.

 Husband and I wanted to make sure that our eldest knew what was expected of her regarding pet care, so we had a long talk with her about her obligations as a pet owner.

Making it clear that it would be her sole responsibility to feed, clean out and generally look after her new pet. She assured us she was mature enough to do what was necessary and that it was her dream and that we had nothing to worry about. She was 7 years old. What fool takes the word of a 7 year old? Us apparently. Not that it bothered Husband in the slightest because all undone pet type jobs fell conveniently *for him* under my job description.

Wife / Mother job description-
*Cook
*Cleaner (in a fashion)
*Dog poo picker upper
*Dog feeder and walker
*Lizard carer
*Holiday organiser
*General admin person
*School admin person
*Bank admin person
*General slave

And now it seems I can add to the list-
*Small pet cleaner outer
*Small pet feeder
*Small pet playmate

*Small pet prime care giver, and overall saviour in the rabbit world.

He was introduced to his new mansion that had now acquired its own outside space. We had purchased some metal fencing that pushed into the grass and linked together making his own secure garden. It had also been discussed and decided that we would take some security measures out on our Bully. We bought a long chain (the narrow flimsy kind, not the thick heavy mean stuff), that he would be hooked on to when he was outside unattended. This would help me out by not having to supervise outdoor activities 24-7 and hopefully avoid a repeat performance of the guinea pig incident.

I don't want to take all the credit for keeping him alive. Our Anklebiter did her bit now and again, maybe twice or three times in total. I actually didn't mind doing it for the most part except for the cleaning out. I wasn't that fond of it because the hutch attracted these freakish spiders with tiny bodies and long spindly legs that creeped me right out. A few weeks went by without any drama. No real drama anyway. It came to light following a couple of episodes that this rabbit we had hand selected after rigorous criteria testing was an escape artist. His ninja-like abilities were a little unexpected and saw us begin to call him 'The secret agent' because of his stealthiness. On more than one occasion we had found him outside his cage on the other side of the fence in the field next door with no idea how he got there. It was a miracle he never disappeared completely. Shortly after these bungled escape attempts it came to my attention that true to his sneaky nature, the rabbit was hiding a dirty little secret.

'The Secret Agent' had fleas.

Oh my Fucking God.

I was sharing a morning cuddle with him before putting him in his garden run when during a little head stroke I noticed about a thousand million trillion of the tiniest little black things scurrying around between his eyes and around his ears.

I wanted to die.

I don't do well with things like this. Up until this time I'd never had to deal with fleas. Our dog had never had fleas as I went to great lengths to prevent even a sniff of an itch because I knew if it ever happened it would be my unravelling. Thinking about the times I'd held 'The Secret Agent' and the clothes I'd worn and wondering if I'd transferred the fleas to the house, maybe in the carpets or towels or cushions made me feel physically sick. I had a couple of options.

> 1. Release the rabbit into the field, make it look like another escape and hope it ran away and didn't hang around the fence this time, then burn the house to the ground on the off chance a flea had got loose in there.

OR

> 2. Flea treat the rabbit and uncover the origins of the fleas whilst also treating the house on the off chance a flea had got loose and had started a nest in one of the settees.

It was a very close call. Unsure if I'd made the right decision I reluctantly went with option 2.

For the longest week of my life I bathed him everyday in flea shampoo and combed out the dead ones. I deep cleaned everything within the walls of my home that resembled a soft furnishing and must have spent about £100 on endless bottles of industrial strength flea spray. I was worn out, felt frazzled and quite close to the edge. Some would say it was all unnecessary and over the top but as we all know, once something worms its way into your psyche it can be hard to dislodge it. After an intricate investigation and many long hours spying out of the window at the hutch, mostly with snacks because that's what you do on a stakeout, I've seen it on TV, it became apparent how he had caught fleas. As dusk approached each evening so did the wild rabbits that wandered freely in the woods surrounding our house. Encasing the hutch there were six or seven of them. Conversing through the mesh at the bottom half of the cage, I'm certain they were the ones that broke him out on his escape attempts. They were his friends but unfortunately I had to put a stop to it. I couldn't risk another flea infestation. The mere thought of it made me feel weak. Husband had his instructions to invent something to keep the wild ones out and 'The

Secret Agent' in. He did this by cleverly lifting the cage onto a stack of bricks so the wild rabbits wouldn't be able to reach the hutch. They would have to settle for waving to each other instead and let that be enough.

With the departure of the fleas and the modification to the rabbit mansion I thought we had turned a corner. At this point the rabbit's life expectancy had exceeded all expectations. Our Bully had been relatively well behaved and our house was still standing (thanks to me choosing option 2 and not option 1). Anklebiter was super happy with her choice of pet and life was good.

The day of the Murder
On the morning of the day we never speak of, it was warm and the sun was hazy with not much breeze. A typical September day. 'The Secret Agent' had been part of our family for close to 2 months. I'd dropped both Anklebiters at school armed with PE kits, packed lunches and extra clothes for playing out on the field which the school liked to turn into an actual lesson and called it 'Forest Schools'. Following a quick whip around Asda I put away the shopping

which left me time to walk and feed the dog before I let out the rabbit.

'The Secret Agent' and I had our usual flea free morning cuddle before I refilled his food, changed his water and put him in his small scale gated private garden. The chain we had got especially for our Bully was on the fence at the back of the house in a separate area. He couldn't see the hutch or rabbit garden at all as I thought that it might ease the temptation, and so far it had worked brilliantly. Out of sight, out of mind as they say. I hooked him onto it as I had done previous mornings leaving him the freedom of about 10 metres to mooch about and sunbath. He only ever spent an hour at a time tied up because I didn't like the idea, not when he was used to free reign over both gardens and the woods at the side of our house. It was usual for me to go about my day's jobs and check on the animals about every 15-20 minutes to make sure everyone was keeping their noses clean and out of trouble. Jamie Oliver's cookbook was on my lap and a cuppa was in my hand as I deliberated what to do for tea. There were so many recipes it was difficult to choose. I was so engrossed that it suddenly dawned on me I hadn't spot checked things outside. Nothing a quick look out of the kitchen window wouldn't fix. Except that when I looked outside, all that greeted me was a dogless garden and chain laying on the grass lifelessly with a collar on the end but definitely no dog.

WAS THIS A SICK JOKE?

Horror swept through my body along with that sick feeling that rushes down to your toes and back up to your stomach making you instantly need a poo. Sweating like a bitch, feeling close to passing out I ventured to the lounge window that overlooked the hutch. Not only was there no 'Secret Agent' in the fenced rabbit run but the metal sections were now all flat on the floor, no longer resembling a fence. Rushing out of the front door frantically looking for both animals I started to imagine the chase that had ensued. Our Bully, hot on the heels of the ninja that was 'The Secret Agent'. Surely with stealth skills possessed by no other rabbit he'd more than likely be up a tree somewhere blowing raspberries and taunting our dog about his lack of catching and climbing skills. As I was wondering which tree to search first my eye was drawn to the Anklebiters trampoline, or under it to be more accurate. The scene I took in ripped my breath from my body, and all emotion it seemed because I froze and stood there staring open mouthed for what seemed like an awfully long time.

Under the trampoline sat our dog, tail wagging with the biggest grin on his face. He had never looked so pleased with himself. His whole face was soaked in blood and next to him laid 'The secret Agent', who didn't have to worry anymore about his identity being revealed on secret missions because he now had no head.

OOOHHH FUUUCK.

Out of a lot of scenarios that had played out in my head this was not an ideal one. What should I do? How would I clean it up? How would I conceal all of this from every other member of the family, especially the eldest Anklebiter? All questions that must run through the head of a killer once they have committed a murder. I hadn't murdered our rabbit but our Bully had and now I was left to sort it out but I didn't want to. He was making me an accomplice. I wanted to jump out of a top floor window or design and build a time machine within an hour or blink three times and it all disappear, or do anything at all that wasn't dealing with this carnage.

The murderer, our Bully, was frogmarched to the outside tap where I cleaned off all the evidence from his face before putting him in the house. Then before removing the headless body or tackling the blood stain on the grass, I sat calmly like a total psychopath and drank a cup of tea pondering my next move. By the time I'd gathered myself enough to complete the clean up phase, it was an hour before school pick up, I had to get moving. The plan was to cloak the body in a carrier bag and then to use nearly a full reel of duct tape to assure no peeping eyes or nimble fingers would uncover what was lurking beneath. The duct tape parcel would then be housed in an old shoe box which would in turn also have another full reel of duct tape wrapped around it to secure it. Having a plan and carrying it out are two different things it would appear. For approximately half an hour I hovered over the body up close, carrier bag in hand and wearing a gardening glove. It was a real struggle but eventually I forced myself to pick him up and put him in the bag, apologising to him the whole time and telling him how much we loved him. If there had been any onlookers it would have definitely confirmed suspicions about the slightly odd, crazy lady that lived in the house near the woods.

The box containing the body was hidden behind the hutch, the blood stained grass had been washed with soapy water but was still discoloured so I put a miniature camping chair on what was left of the stain, obscuring it awkwardly under the trampoline. A desperate attempt to conceal the events that happened there earlier. I'd decided almost immediately that I would tell our Anklebiter a small white lie. She would be devastated enough without adding a further burden of the truth. I would leave it until the next day then tell her I'd found him in his hutch and that he had died during the night peacefully in his sleep due to a mysterious sudden illness. The thought of explaining to Husband that our little furry friend had been callously slaughtered on my watch was a different kettle of fish, and not sitting well at all. He would blame me, like I'd done it on purpose, and I wouldn't hear the end of it for weeks. Bearing this in mind there were a few possible scenarios that I was working on.

Going over it in my mind again and again, trying to talk myself into the lies I'd created about what happened I was getting nowhere fast. I'd narrowed it down, and would use one of the following

1. An eagle swooped down and seized 'The Secret Agent 'from his rabbit pen, carrying him off and rendering me helpless.

2. He succeeded on one of his many escape attempts, climbed a tree and fell out, breaking his neck.

3. He had a heart attack which made his head fall off.

These were my most believable ones. My real problem was I wasn't very good at lying. My voice becomes strangely high pitched and my lip twitches at the edge. If by some miracle the person I'm lying to doesn't notice these little gems there's a very good chance the guilt will become too much and I will confess everything mid lie, which I admit is weird but has happened on occasion. For example, once when I'd been caught speeding by one of those sneaky police vans I'd received a notice through the post informing me of the intended prosecution against me unless I considered a speeding seminar. A no brainer, of course I'd attend the seminar but under no circumstances could Husband know about it. He always told me I drove too fast. I always told him to shut up and mind his own business. There was no way I was going to admit to not only being wrong but also being caught. As part of this offer there was a fairly hefty fine to pay as well. A complete waste of money, that he'd earned, he would say. Apparently I don't value money because I'm not the main breadwinner which means I deliberately waste money, spending it willy nilly because I know he has to pay for things and not me. Luckily the seminar had fallen on a Friday, one of my work days. Perfect. I booked a half day's holiday and would return to work afterwards, I would tell no one, stealth would be my middle name and Husband would be none the wiser. A sterling plan. Or it would have been if I hadn't caved on the day and actually rang him from the seminar to admit everything over the phone. After weeks of feeling uneasy about what I was planning, I'd actually made it to the day of the speeding course. I was home and dry, then for no reason other than my own guilt I spilled my guts.

BACK TO THE MURDER

After thinking constantly about which lie I would tell and which sounded most credible, my brain had turned to mush and could no longer decipher what was good and what wasn't. Not that it mattered in the slightest because I knew without a shadow of a doubt that the moment Husband looked at me I'd tell him everything.

The Anklebiters were playing inside while I stood on the front doorstep dancing around like I had ants in my pants waiting for Husband to get in from work. The guilt was eating its way out and I couldn't stand it. I wanted it off my chest and over and done with.

As Husband parked up the car I ran over to the drivers side and as he cracked the door to get out I blurted, 'There's been an accident. The dog got loose and ate the rabbit's head and now he's dead.' Husband was looking at me like he'd just found out I used to be a man. **I've never been a man, just to be clear.**

'WHAAAAT?!' He said slowly, shaking his head in disbelief, 'the rabbit and the dog are dead?'

'No, not the dog, just the rabbit.' I answered triumphantly, like I was delivering some good news. I explained the whole horrific ordeal. And absolutely on cue and as predicted by me, the woman who knows everything, after a few groans and a bit of head holding, he blamed me. He even went as far as to call ME a murderer. Apparently it was a ridiculous move to have the dog on his chain while the rabbit was out, and to be fair as he was saying it, I was in full agreement. It had been maybe a tiny bit irresponsible but I wasn't letting him know that I agreed. When we told our Anklebiter that her beloved pet had gone to heaven she was upset beyond measure as I knew she would be. When she asked what he had died of, I told her he had been poorly. As the words left my mouth I could see out of the corner of my eye Husband glaring at me. 'Poorly?' He mouthed at me so the Anklebiter wouldn't hear.

'You dont get more poorly than not having a head.' I mouthed back.

The whole family was present for the burial ceremony that our Anklebiter had insisted on. She had written a poem and drawn a RIP picture to pin to the tree next to where he would be buried. It was very sweet. Ironically it featured drawings of both the rabbit and the dog with the caption underneath 'Best Friends'. I produced the shoe box that held 'The Secret Agents' little headless body and that was now nearly entirely covered in duct tape. Our smallest Anklebiter was 5 at the time and was obsessed with all things dead, as a lot of small boys (and serial killers) are at that age. As soon as he saw the shoe box he asked to see the dead body. I explained that we couldn't do that because it would be too upsetting and the box was also taped up quite well. He told me that it didn't matter, he'd just come back tomorrow and dig it up. Trying hard to hide my horror I shushed him and made sure that the grave stone Husband put over the fresh grave was gigantic, and far too heavy for a 5 year old to shift. Husband didn't speak to me properly for around 2 weeks and when he did he referred to me as 'The Murderer'.

We don't ever speak of what happened that day. This is because I don't want to remind

Husband that I was an accomplice to murder but mainly because our eldest Anklebiter still doesnt know the true story and I'd like to keep it that way.

The Drug Dealers Villa

Summer holidays are always something I look forward to. The two weeks of the year I'm free from mentally juggling finance and admin and Husband's grumpiness. We usually opt for a villa so that once they are fenced in, the children are at liberty to run wild and free, *no change there then.*

This particular year, for one reason or another we had left it late and I was worried we wouldn't get anywhere decent. Gone were the days of slumming it amongst the cockroaches and pull out beds. These days we liked to go places that had at least the same level of home comfort that we were used to. So it was left to me as it was every year. Having done my stint as a travel agent in my younger years I liked to think I was still a master in this field and was only happy when I could unearth the most outrageously good deals.

27 nights in a luxurious 5 * Spanish villa
4 bedrooms

4 bathrooms
Private infinity pool and jacuzzi
Beachfront location
Butler
Private chef
Personal masseuse
Local return flights
Car hire
TOTAL COST £199

Now that's what I'm talking about.
'Bullshit,' I hear you cry, and you're right. But this was the sort of deal I was always striving for.

Surprisingly, *or not so much*, I never found this particular deal. However I had managed to find something that I didn't think was bad given it was due to leave in 3 weeks and it was prime time holiday season just before the start of the summer holidays. I know that particular week is chosen by a lot of parents so they can save a few extra quid. By having their child feign illness in order to be excused from school a few days before the summer holidays start they avoid the sharp increase in price that happens the day school breaks up. Genius.

11 nights in a private Spanish villa. Exclusive use of the ground floor and private pool.
2 bedrooms
1 bathroom
Must arrange own flights
Owner, who occupies the first floor away for most of the summer.
TOTAL COST £1200

Not as great as the first deal but as that one was a total fabrication, and I'd been trawling the net for 3 days without even a sniff of anything suitable I had a choice to make. Also possibly a small point to note was that this property only had 3 reviews. They weren't bad but were very short and not articulated particularly well. I'm usually massive on reviews. Must be at least 4 out of 5 stars and have over a hundred reviewers. My options here were limited. I decided that a holiday in the sun was better than no holiday at all. I had to have this one. I was on it like a car bonnet.

After confirming our holiday and paying in full I received a message from the owner. He thanked me for booking and advised me that he would be flying to Morocco the day after we arrived so he would be available to collect us from the airport for a small additional charge if we wished. It was one less thing for me to book separately and one less headache to worry about so I accepted. I noticed during this correspondence that the English was a bit pigeony and somewhere down the line I'd realised that his name sounded Dutch. Surely Dutch people knew as much about renting villas as the next person. I wasn't concerned.

The Day of Departure

It had been a smooth flight with the usual hurdles. As I had booked the flights fairly close to the departure date we had only just managed to get the last few seats. Unfortunately, *or fortunately if you are Husband,* this meant we couldn't all sit together. It's usually the airline's policy that if you are travelling with small children they do some seat shuffling to prevent little ones sitting alone, next to total strangers, resulting in them crying all the way there and annoying the living shit out of the entire flight. Due to this we had been allocated 2 lots of 2 seats. Quicker than the speed of light Husband had selected our older child who was 6 at the time. Very mature and capable for her age I knew she would make small talk with other passengers, showing off her charm and maturity she would without doubt be a hit with everyone in her section of the plane. Therefore leaving Husband free to read, relax and have a lovely time.

This left me with our 3 year old son. For all mothers who have travelled on a flight with a tired 3 year old and no help, **thanks very much Husband,** I don't believe I have to explain further. Suffice to say that when we touched down in Spain it was not a moment too soon. Had it been a moment longer I would have attempted to drown myself in the paper cup of lukewarm tea I'd been nursing for the last 2 hours. **Lazy flight attendants.**

The flight was a few minutes late. It was 10.05am and the airport was super busy but as I'd sorted the transfer with the owner like the super efficient award winning wife I was, we were set. It was just a case of locating him.

An hour passed. **FFS.** The airport was no longer busy and there were hardly any taxi transfer people left waiting for late arrivals. We stood in silence. I looked at Husband. He looked at me. Our faces expressionless.

Pissed off. I had rang the contact number Dutch had given me 20 times since we arrived but it continued to go straight to answerphone. On the cusp of a breakdown I saw something near the escalator.

You know in action films when everything goes into slow motion and the hero of the moment is running away from an explosion? Well I could see someone tearing through the airport in what seemed like the same kind of slo mo, except it wasn't a hero. It was a tall, tanned man. His clothes were soaked, he was sweating so much he looked as though he'd taken a fully clothed swim and was just beginning to dry out.

And there he was.

Over an hour late, sweating like a peaodo on the school run and stinking of weed. And not an apology in sight.

That was Dutch. Our host. **Brilliant.**

As he led us towards the brown transit van, small talk was at a minimum. He was visibly struggling to negotiate himself and it was plain to see that he was coming down from a good night out. The sliding door on one side of the van had been completely battered in. Probably the result of a crash that hadn't been repaired. As Husband opened the front door the stench of weed flooded out. It was rancid. **3 fucking reviews. I'd asked for this.** The journey to the villa had been uncomfortable to put it politely. Trying to avoid Husband's death stare while willing the children not to breathe for the whole time we were trapped amongst the weed fumes, I was relieved when we pulled up at the gate of the villa. On entry instead of being bowled over by its beauty all we saw was a load of workmen, a dug up garden and a luminous green sludgy swimming pool that hadnt had a clean for the best part of 10 years.

I was speechless. Gutted. *I knew this would happen to me. How could it not.*

Looking at Husband I could see he was horrified. The children being small didn't understand any of this except we were at a house with a pool in the sun. They were very excited. Dutch had found his voice by now and seemed to have recovered slightly, enough to boast about his wonderful villa. We followed him inside through the patio door.

Holy Fucking Mother of God.

We were faced with what can only be described as a filthy smack hole. It hadn't been cleaned in months. There was inch thick dust on the kitchen worktops, unemptied ashtrays, a smashed mirrored wardrobe in the bedroom next to the piss stained mattress and pillows. No pillow cases. No duvet cover. No hope.

I wanted to cry. As I turned to Husband, out of the corner of my eye I saw the children excitedly raking through one of the cases they had opened when we weren't looking. The eldest was already in her butterfly swimming cozzy and was currently trying to locate her brother's trunks amongst the rest of the clothes. Not seeing any way we could stay, I hurried over to them trying to discourage the outfit changes that seemed to be happening.

It's not a regular occurrence that I am lost for words. But this time I was. Lost for words and lost in general. It was all such a shock. Now this was very disappointing. When people talk about what they excel at, their strengths, for years I could never really think of anything specific for myself until I slowly realised, after a few incidents, that I was good in a crisis. That was my strength. Except this time I had crashed and burned. Following around that pothead, saying absolutely nothing like a mute, I needed to take action but words evaded me.

Thank God for Husband.

Husband. Not usually one to keep his temper and negotiate with people. Usually the one to lose his temper, shout obscenities, strangle the target with a choke hold and ask questions later.

As I was shovelling our clothes that now littered the patio, back into the suitcase I could hear Husband and Dutch having a heated debate about the shitty arse pool and the disgusting state of the villa. I held my breath. I knew what was coming next. I was familiar with the gurgling sound a person makes when they're being strangled to within an inch of their life. Any. Second. Now. But it never came. **What was going on here? I was in unknown territory.**

'Come on we're off, get the kids and I'll get the cases.' Said Husband gruffly through gritted teeth, stalking towards me. He was currently 9 foot tall and the veins in his neck were protruding. He often resembled the incredible Hulk when he was angry but I was amazed that he'd managed not to 'Hulk smash' Dutch today. I was very proud.

'We're going on an adventure. Follow me,' Husband told the children.

They were so excited at the prospect of an adventure. Shrieking and laughing they skipped after him and I brought up the rear. The villa had been on the Pueblo in the mountains so we followed the winding coast road all the way down to the sea front. It was miles. At least 5 I bet. On route we had met an expat in his mid 60's called Arthur. He was on his daily walk and had mistaken our good morning greeting as an invitation to deliver his full life story. He was a talker but he seemed nice and sympathised with our situation. He confirmed that if we continued on the coastal road we would eventually come across a hotel. **Thank God. In the dry heat of the midday sun coupled with the stress of this whole debacle, I felt like I might die quite soon but**

I was trying to hold it together for everyone. It was nearly 30 degrees and it had taken us close to 3 hours to get to the hotel at the end of the coast road with 2 ankle biters and 3 suitcases but bugger me sideways with a fish fork we'd done it! We walked into the hotel Arthur had promised us and tried to book a room. As we approached the front reception desk I could see a large sign sat on the counter which read;

'Online bookings only.'

Fuck right off.

As Husband and I battled to gain access to the 30 minutes free wifi we had been guaranteed to get with buying a meal I could feel the life force being sucked out of me. All I wanted was to get rid of these cases, get a shower and change my clothes. I was sweating my tits off and was beginning to be able to smell myself.

Come on, we've all been there.

I think you'll agree there's nothing more off putting than trying to enjoy your lunch with the smell of fanny filling your nostrils. **Just saying.**

It seemed to be a lost cause. For some reason our phones just wouldn't connect. We'd never had any problems previously, at home or abroad but now, when we were in dire straits and our sanity and possibly our lives depended on it, they refused to work. Just as I looked out of the window, **checking to see if it was high enough to jump out of,** low and behold who was looking back at me but Arthur. Our exercise loving, life story telling, English speaking Arthur. **Thank you thank you thank you.**

Following a brief explanation of the events that had happened over the last 2 hours, Arthur insisted we go home with him to his apartment that was apparently less than a 5 minute walk away. He continued to insist that once we were there he could offer us a cold drink, a shady balcony and full internet access on his laptop to book some accommodation.

Arthur the saviour.
Or ...
Arthur the mad axe killer?

We didn't know him, he could have been anyone. This thought began to dawn on me on the walk over there. I couldn't stop thinking about it and began to convince myself that we would be his next victims. Due to this thought my tit sweats were getting out of hand and I felt more anxious by the minute. I kept trying to catch Husband's eye, to alert him to my theory and now and again he did look right at me, only to look away again blowing out his cheeks and letting air slowly out of his mouth.

He was cross. Cross I'd booked a wank villa. Cross we had been forced to walk 350 miles, **actually 5**, in the scorching heat. Cross we couldn't book in at the hotel while we were actually standing in it, and now, cross that we were going willingly with a mad axe killer to meet our doom.

The apartment was small ,cosy and well decorated. Arthur took out a pitcher of lemon cordial from the fridge and directed me to the corner of the room where there was a small desk with a laptop perched on top. 'Help yourself love,' he gestured to the chromebook, 'there's no password on it.'

I accessed google and started a search for hotels in the area. Arthur had offered to drive us to wherever we decided to book so not to limit us to the immediate area. Given the short notice we might not have had a great deal of choice. 'Let's leave mum to book something nice. Would you two like to go and see the swimming pool?' Arthur asked the children. I looked at Husband with wide eyes and clenched teeth.

Quickly Husband jumped in, 'I'd love to see the pool Arthur, come on kids.' Quietly taking their hands he and the Anklebiters followed Arthur out of the front door and up the ramp towards the communal pool leaving me to secure us a nice place to stay. Had Arthur really expected to take the children out unsupervised when we had only just met? You can't be too careful in this world we live in, full of dangerous situations and strange people. But maybe he was just a nice man and not a murderer at all. Only time would tell. After all, he had just left me, a total stranger, in his home unattended. How did he know I wasn't going to steal all the best silver? My thoughts were interrupted by the sound of Husband's voice frantically calling out our son's name over and over again. When I reached the front door to see what all the commotion was I saw Husband carrying our daughter, both crying and him still calling out.

WHERE WAS MY SON?

My stomach dropped. I felt sick. My beautiful little boy. Where was he? I could feel the panic rising up to my chest, then Husband spoke. I turned around for a minute and when I looked back he was gone. I've been shouting for him and have looked everywhere but he's nowhere.' The desperation and defeat in his voice was overwhelming. 'I came back here because I thought he might have tried to find his way back to you but …' His voice trailed off. He looked broken. A level of calm swept over me. The sort of strength and focus that I had when I birthed him.

    'Go back and keep shouting and looking, I'll stay here in case he comes back,' I said, slipping into crisis mode. I took my daughter and held her while I continued to shout from the front door and the balcony. Husband ran back to continue the search near the pool. What seemed like an eternity later I saw Husband running down the ramp that led to the pool clutching a crying child. My child.

Thank God.

My baby had recently been going through a faze of hiding, as many children his age do. It turned out that he had been climbing on something around the pool he shouldn't have been and Husband had asked him to stop it. Feeling annoyed at being told off he had walked down one of 4 flights of stone stairs in the cliff face and hidden. When he heard Husband and Arthur frantically calling his name he had tried to find his way back but was confused as to which set of stairs he should take. Luckily there was a Spanish teenager that he approached for help. The teenager understood and took him back to Husband.

Someone or something must have been looking out for us that day because this scenario could have easily had a different ending. We thanked our lucky stars and we thanked Arthur for his kindness and hospitality **and for not being a machete wielding maniac,** as he dropped us off at our new hotel.

Hopefully now our holiday could start. Continue. And end. All without any more drama.

After a very dodgy start we had one of our best holidays. The place was lovely. A small authentic Spanish apartment block that was mostly occupied by locals on their summer jollies. We had the pool area to ourselves during the daytime and watched it come to life on an evening in line with Spanish culture. A small cove of beach a two minute walk away was where we spent our mornings after we'd eaten the freshly baked croissants from the shop outside. I have some lovely memories of this holiday, some weird ones and also some scary ones. But I suppose that's life.

Also, mid holiday I started to receive some very strange Whatsapp messages from Dutch. Clearly smacked off his tits on whatever he made regular trips to Morocco for, he kept sending videos with a running commentary of the villa after he'd attempted to clean it up. In his thick Dutch accent he would tell us how 'beeeeeautiful' the villa was and how he wanted to show us what we were missing! How the pool, **now with less floating sludgy bits,** was the 'most beautiful pool in the whole of spain!' How perfect everything was and that he bet we were sorry we had left! It really made us laugh and just added to the great memories that were made that year.

Shiatsu Practitioner Or Professional Sexual Predator?

I've suffered with my back intermittently for the last 10 years. Sometimes it's my lower back, sometimes my upper back and neck, but more often than not it's usually a God awful pain between my shoulder blades that I just can't shake off. I've tried a few things to remedy it but have never committed to one thing long enough to know if it works. Exercise can do the trick occasionally. Sometimes I get the exercise bug which could be a flash in the pan at a week, or it could be as long and drawn out as 6 months before it bites the dust along with the good intentions. The pain definitely eases when I make the effort to do it and although I'm acutely aware that the minute I stop prancing around with Jane Fonda the back pain will return, I still stop. **Jane Fonda must be 80 years old by now. Is it wrong to covet an 80 year old's body? Asking for a friend.**

To be clear I am not to be mistaken for someone who enjoys exercise. I dislike sweating and being short of breath. I'm one of those who has to lay down for a bit after scaling 2 flights of stairs. I hate anything physically demanding to the point where I can usually talk myself out of whatever I'm contemplating, thanks to far fetched fabrications I have invented as to why it wouldn't be wise. When I eventually become focused and in the throes of an exercise spurt, in addition to Jane, I might also partake in Shaun T's insanity workouts which I can confirm are undoubtedly insane, but quite satisfying **(once you've finished)**. I'm also partial to a spot of spinning. A totally pointless cycling exercise in which a gang of crazy people pedal like shit off a stick and sweat like holy fuck on a set of bikes that are bolted to the floor and go nowhere, making the cyclist so breathless they question if a stroke is iminnant. The bike itself has a dial that can be twisted to increase or decrease intensity which you are left in charge of with the understanding you must push yourself and test your limits and not have it on the easiest setting to mimic a sunday afternoon jolly in the park. The sadist trying to pass himself off as the instructor, who is actually the devil himself, is found sitting on a cycle at the front of the class shouting at the participants in a Sergeant Major voice, waiting for the moment when some poor bugger who can't keep up *(usually me),* slows down in the nick of time to prevent an actual heart attack, so he can single them out and humiliate them. It's very fulfilling. It's actually a strange thing because even though I despise every living second of the class for the duration, imagining ways to 'off' the personal trainer in charge, as soon as it's over I can't wait to book in for the next one. It's weirdly addictive.

Having not done an exercise stint for a while and my back pain being particularly bad I needed to work out what my options were and what my next move would be. Once I had whittled it down and randomly chosen a route to pursue, probably with no rational thought, the likelihood of giving up after a few days being particularly high, I would move on to the next route and so forth. I would perhaps leap around with Jane a few times in between but my heart wouldn't be in it. That was the usual procedure.

I was at Mums and had been bending her ear about the agony my back was putting me through. We were discussing the merits of Shiatsu Healing.

One of the Work Girls had recently been to see a practitioner and had sung her praises from the rooftops so this was obviously top of the options list.

'What is Shitaki healing anyway?' Asked Mum.
'Shiatsu Healing,' I corrected, 'shitaki is a type of mushroom.' Unperturbed, she continued, 'I have heard of it when I went to Singapore with Auntie, but I'm not sure what they actually do?'
'It's a sort of back massage I think. They realign your vertebrae to cure all sorts of pain and ailments. It originated in Japan,' I replied.
'You should go and see that back man I went to. Might loosen you up and help the pain?' Mum offered.
'Is he any good?' I asked.
'He did wonders for my back. I think he's a perv though.' Said Mum matter of factly.
'What do you mean? Did he do things he shouldn't have?' I asked, shocked at her revelation and ready to call the police.

'No but he was creepy. Really creepy. Wouldn't surprise me if it came out that he'd jumped on someone.' She responded.

Mum could always be relied upon to recommend a good hairdresser, an experienced nail technician or a professional sexual predator undercover as a chiropractor it would seem. Not only did she have suspicions he was a closet rapist waiting in the wings to attack a carefully selected victim but she was trying to get me to book in with him. **Thanks very much Mum, tempting but I think I'll pass.**

This sealed the deal for me. The first thing on my jobs list for the next day was to ring the mushroom lady and make an appointment.

The Next Day
I dialled the number I'd been given. The phone rang and was answered almost immediately. 'Hello,' said a breathless voice on the other end of the phone.
   'Oh hello, I've been told you might be able to help me with my back and wondered if I could book an appointment please?' I began.

'Err yes, fine.' A pause. 'Can you come now?' she spat.

'I'm sorry I have plans today, I was hoping you might be free on Thursday?' I replied.

Not waiting for me to finish she said, 'Yes 1pm if that suits you. I'll see you then.'

I got the impression she was about to hang up so I quickly asked for her address and told her my name. A very basic thing but we hadn't bothered with any niceties at all. She didn't even ask who had recommended me. She had just invited me to her home with no prior knowledge of me at all and no idea if I would bop her over the head when she wasn't looking and rob her blind. She seemed nice.

I arrived at the given address on the given day and was greeted at the door by a seventy something lady of delicate proportions. Unsure if she would have the physical strength I assumed it took to manipulate my spine to its original setting, I went as directed into what I suspected was her therapy room.

'We'll soon get rid of that pain between your shoulder blades,' she announced. I hadn't said a word about anything since arriving a whole

10 seconds ago and I hadn't had the chance on the phone. Maybe Shiatsu practitioners were also psychic? The smell that had welcomed me as I crossed the threshold was not diminishing and only led me to believe she must be housing 1000 dogs in her kitchen. The room itself was an OCD clean freaks' worst nightmare. A scabby old mattress with what I concluded was one of the dogs blankets' thrown haphazardly over it was abandoned in the middle of the room and was surrounded by bags, clothes and numerous dusty books similar to what I have seen on hoarder programs.

I thought it was only good manners to introduce myself. 'Hi I'm . . .' But she didn't appear to be interested if I was her client or a door to door saleswoman.
 'Lay down. Face down, arms by your sides.' She instructed, cutting me off and pointing at the health hazard of a mattress.

I wondered if she might want to know what my complaint was or ask about any medical history but that didn't seem to be at the forefront of her mind but then I suppose if you are a mind reader you have the advantage of not having to ask any questions. I followed her orders.

As I laid face down, trying not to breath in the germs on the blanket, I felt her mount me. WTF was happening here? Rubbing my back vigorously she explained that once my muscles were warm enough she would apply pressure to certain points in my back and when she did this I would be required to take a deep breath and to blow it out when she told me to, while she applied the pressure. Fair enough.

'Breathe in and ... OUT!'

It felt like 10 men had jumped on my back in unison. Along with my involuntary grunt there was an almighty crack! She did this 3 more times in quick succession at various points between my neck and lower back. I'm not going to lie, it was a massive shock to the system but very satisfying.

'That shoulder blade of yours is being a bugger,' she said, not mincing her words. 'Sit on your bottom, legs out in front and hands behind your head.' She approached me from behind and took a firm grasp of my elbows which were stuck out each side of my head like a bird ready to land. She continued 'You're not going to like this and it will hurt. Now when I say breathe out, do it.' I was terrified and felt like I might need to change my undergarments quite soon.

Breath in and ... OUT!'

I followed her demands to the letter. I daren't do anything else. On this command she wrenched both my elbows backwards and stuck her knee in my back. A huge pop from my back and scream that came from me, escaped into the room. She was right, it did hurt but it was the shock of it that threw me more.

'Lovely. That's back where it should be now.' She barked, clearly pleased with efforts.

 From the floor she told me to lay face up on the other therapy bed that was higher but still as hygienically questionable. In turn, she brought each of my legs across my body and at just the right time gave a firm yank, and was again rewarded with loud multiple clicking sounds. Swiftly moving to my head she stood behind me. I couldn't see her but I found out only too quickly what she was up to. Grasping my chin and the top of my head she snapped my head first one way and then the other, with no warning. It was awful and I honestly thought for a split second someone must have paid her to take me out. I don't mean take me out for coffee, I mean like a professional hit. Like in the films when a professional assassin grabs the head of his target and quickly twists it, breaking their neck instantly. My money was on Husband. I couldn't think of anyone else I'd annoyed lately, not enough to warrant a bounty on my head anyway. Interrupting my thoughts I heard a voice say, 'All done. Your shoulder, hip and neck all went back very nicely. I'm surprised you've been walking around as easily as you have with your neck being like that. It must have been out since childhood. Go and sit in the massage chair for 10minutes.'

This could only mean I was still alive and hadn't actually been assassinated. Her little speech would also indicate she really was realigning my neck and not attempting murder. Thank God for that.

It became apparent very quickly that she was actually a lovely woman. Her earlier briskness I can only guess came from wanting to get the job done, and finished before my muscles cooled down. In the 10 minutes I sat in the massage chair I learned about her family, her neighbours, her charity work and the entire history from word dot regarding the origins of Shiatsu practices, even down to the monks it was performed on in the monasteries hundreds of years before. It was very enlightening, and very relaxing. Coupled with the massage chair I had to fight hard not to bob off to sleep. I walked out of there a new woman, or at least a woman with a new back. Although the feeling of soreness engulfed my body, the actual aches and pains had gone. I only hoped it wasn't a temporary thing. On seeing me out she explained that she wasn't as nimble or strong as she used to be so it might be necessary for me to make a return visit if after a few days there was still any pain. I thanked the lovely mushroom lady, hopefully conveying just how grateful I was that she had been able to release me from my pain. I felt loose and much taller than my 5ft 6 inches. I never gave it away that under no circumstances would I be returning whether the pain came back or my arm or head fell off or not. I just dont think I could go through the neck snapping part again.

I popped in at Mums on the way home to report that in my opinion Shiatsu healing was definitely the way forward and to inform her that I'd be giving the perv, although highly recommended, a wide berth.

So far my back pain is still much less than it was. My near assasination attempt by a pensioner coupled with a minimal amount of exercise has made me feel like I'm more on top of this issue than I have been in years, so for now I'll plod along doing my thing. In the event that the pain returns in proportions that I can't handle I know without a doubt that I'll book back in with the mushroom lady, if not to fix my back then definitely to put me out of my misery hitman style.

Country Living

The sun was shining, the dogs were playing outside on the lawn just where I could see them in case I had to jump in to referee, and I was guzzling cups of tea like they were going out of fashion. Sitting around the kitchen table I was just about to dig into the luxury chocolate cake that I'd been saving especially for this occasion, a catch up with my cronies. My mouth watering and with all my concentration I sliced into the chocolate mass of yumminess when my friend yelled… 'Ahhhh what's the little dog got? Ahhhh, it's furry and screaming!!'

We all jumped up and peered through the window. On closer inspection our little Frenchie did indeed have something furry clasped between her tiny jaws. It wasn't one of her many cuddly creature toys and it was definitely screaming, well squeaking actually. Quickly opening the patio door to leap out and deal with it she heard me coming, but instead of running away from me she made a bolt towards the open door, I assume trying to bring it inside to show me, like a cat does when it gifts its owner a dazed but still very much alive rodent.

'It's a rat! OMG she's got a rat! Close the door!' My friend shouted, becoming more hysterical. Swiftly rugby tackling the small French Bulldog to the ground just before she crossed the threshold into the kitchen I managed to stick my thumb into the side of her mouth releasing what turned out to be a tiny baby rabbit. A rat indeed, I think it was time for a trip to specsavers for my over excited friend. The baby scampered off unhurt, and when it had wriggled through the fence back into the safety of the woods I released our little dog we lovingly refer to as 'Sprout' due to her size.

'You did well there.' Said my friend, shaking her head and who now seemed to have calmed the fuck down.

Yes I did. That's because this was not my first rodeo.

Living in the countryside for the last 10 years we have had the privilege of seeing lots of wildlife and on many occasions a little more up close and personal than we might have liked.

Rat Babies
Our first dog Bella was a beautiful Mastiff cross that once took it upon herself to empty a nest of rat babies. Husband and I had been pottering around the garden, the dogs were loose and I had noticed Bella slowly walking back and forth between the logpile that we use for firewood and the end of our garden. After the 3rd time she made the trip, curiosity got the better of us, so after paying close attention and watching what she was actually doing we realised with horror she had been slowly but surely picking out newborn rat babies that couldn't have been more than a day old from the nest she had discovered and was depositing them under the tree in the garden. They were super small and pink with closed eyes and despite making the journey in her mouth, appeared to be unharmed. I'm not sure what I was thinking but I tried to rescue them. As I approached slowly, Bella, who was proudly standing over her new children, looked up from her prized possessions and our eyes locked. Never taking her eyes off mine I managed to get to about a metre away when she quite clearly

thought to herself 'You'll never take them from me alive,' before diving in and devouring the lot of them.

JESUS MARY AND JOSEPH.

So there I was witnessing the savage butchery of 5 innocent rat babies.

I suppose if you had to dig out a silver lining to this grim little tale it would be that at least they wouldn't grow up to be full size evil rodent types that would eventually break into our house or garage and then breed at a seriously offensive rate, like the mice did that had managed to sneak in one year.

Billy the Mouse and Friends
We live between two crop fields that house a gazillion field mice. When it comes to harvest time these poor little creatures have their homes mowed down by the combine harvesters and they literally run from the fields looking for cosy new ones. This usually happens around September when the weather is still warm and we have an abundance of windows and sometimes doors open to let the air circulate and keep us cool. Each year if we

aren't careful about policing this there is always the potential that we will have uninvited guests. Which is exactly what happened the particular year in question.

One morning I stumbled upon a few chocolate ice cream sprinkles on the lightwood laminate in the kitchen. No one eats these in our house, I know this because I don't ever buy them and so it was concluded that these ice cream decorations were in fact mouse poo's. I also discovered much of the same in the cupboard under the sink, further supporting this theory. I used to have horses during my childhood and spent many a summer evening on the yard catching and playing with field mice and having to set the resident Jack Russel on a few stable rats, so rodents didn't bother me. However, small incontinent creatures roaming free in my home pissing at will over all available work surfaces used for food preparation did. With this in mind Husband and I leapt into action and formulated a cunning plan. The cunning we displayed was mind blowing.

We set traps.

The first night of the mission the traps were out and Husband and I were undercover as innocent film watchers in the dark, the room only slightly lit by the light from the TV. It didn't take long before something caught my eye. A quick flash along the skirting board and I knew it would only be a matter of seconds before the familiar 'SNAP' sound of a trap would alert us to the serial pisser's death. Except nothing happened. A few minutes passed and we saw a second flash but this time it was straight in front of us. After focusing in, we realised this rodent was clearly a Billy big bollocks in the mouse world because it was trying to climb onto the settee and continued to do so even after Husband had scrambled for the lightswitch to give us a better view. On further inspection we also discovered that the first mouse was having a lovely meal of peanut butter off the trap and was in no way shape or form dead at all. In fact it was doing a victory dance on top of the trap that had clearly not gone off and was loving every minute of it. After this abysmal effort at critter catching we formulated plan B

Get some better traps.

Within a few days and following a couple of all nighters pulled by Husband and I, we celebrated success because we had eradicated every living thing from our property, except the kids and the dogs. From then on we were very strict about closing doors and only having upstairs windows open. Who knew mice could climb like Edmund Hillary?

Other wildlife we have found in the house include birds, a giant Asian Hornet, a bat and a Queen bumble bee the size of a small horse.

The Soggy Blue Tit
One day I thought our Frenchie had acquired a new soft toy , probably gifted by a family member. Someone is always bringing her something because she's so cute. I took a closer look to see what her newest play thing looked like as she was so enthralled with it. It turned out that it was a bird, a beautiful blue tit. But not of the stuffed variety. Not even of the dead variety, but of the half dazed, half chewed variety. Delightful. It was ejected from the house, and after a heartfelt apology from me, I put it on the fence outside to hopefully dry off and fly away.

The Bat

The bat incident was not so easily dealt with. It had hidden in the house until Husband had left on his annual boys trip away to the Motor GP motorbike racing. Over the years I have discovered that if anything is going to break, go wrong, or get trapped in the house it always waits until Husband has left the county and I am alone and helpless to deal with anything effectively before it strikes. So a few nights into his trip it was practically no surprise at all that a bat was flying around my kitchen like it owned the place. Troops in the form of my Mum and Step dad had to be called in to assist in the bat removal operation, and when they arrived armed with a child's fishing net more suitable to rockpooling than bat catching I knew we were in for a long night. Thankfully it ended in the release of the bat through the patio door. At least that's what we think happened. No one will actually ever really know though because despite my excellent plan for everyone to split up and stand at certain points of the house so we could observe its exact whereabouts at all times, some people who shall remain nameless to avoid all embarrassment, (okay, it was Mum and oldest Anklebiter - sorry, they don't deserve anonymity) abandoned their post at a crucial moment when the bat got too close and ran screaming into the boiler cupboard for safety.

I always like to think it went out the open patio door and didn't disappear into a dark crevice somewhere to hibernate or to die of shock somewhere sneaky. This happened 3 or 4 years ago and I've never come across it so I assume it's not festering anywhere. Fingers crossed.

The Elephant, I mean Hornet
One afternoon I was sitting at the kitchen table enjoying the peace and quiet of an empty house, attempting to do some admin when I heard a motorbike. We live between 2 fields in the country and although there is a road that runs past the top of our driveway it's a good 200 metres from the house so traffic noise was unusual. After a few seconds I realised that the motorbike engine I could hear was actually coming from above our open patio door and on closer inspection saw a wasp the size of an Indian elephant flying around. My blood ran cold. Honestly, what was I meant to do with that? Sweating profusely I watched it intently for what seemed like hours when in fact only a

few minutes had passed. The only action I could muster was to watch it like a hawk and will it with brain power to leave the building whilst I quietly hid behind the utility room door peeping through the crack. Which turned out well because it did actually leave. I must be more powerful than I know. After researching this monstrous creature that had hijacked my kitchen I learnt that it wasn't a wasp on steroids but in fact an Asian hornet, extremely rare in this country and the advice was if you had one at your home you should call the local council to alert them so that they could monitor it and see if it had nested.

Not kill it, but monitor it. **Are you serious?**

Could there really be a nest somewhere with a whole tribe of these monsters lurking in our garden waiting to kill us in our beds? I was taking no chances so a few days later when our little girl came tearing inside from her freshly renovated summer house shrieking and crying about a massive wasp on the window, I had no other option but to send Husband in armed with a steel toe capped boot to wipe it out. I hate killing anything, I've even been known to try and catch blue bottles so they could be released but unfortunately there was no alternative here. It also goes without saying that of course no one set foot in the beautiful play house again. Ever.

I feel it's important to mention that this is by no way an exhaustive list of hairy events that have happened over the years concerning the wildlife we live amongst. I could tell you about when the wild rabbits jump through the chicken wire around our garden and get stuck fast, helpless until we release them, or about the stoats that live in our woodpile that catch enormous hares in the fields that are twice as big as them and what the hares' screams sound like as they are dragged by the neck back to the stoats lair. I could explain how I've had to set up a catch and release system for the huge Queen bees that sometimes find their way into our bedroom through the open window during the summer months and how I know they are there because when they land on the duvet at 3am the bed nearly tips up.

But I won't. It's enough to know that you all now know I have extensive wildlife experience, knowledge and expertise that would rival

Michaela Strachan. In fact I might even go for her job on Springwatch.

Michaela, I'm coming for you.

And then there were three

I've never really liked children. Don't misunderstand, I wouldn't kick one if I saw one on the floor but similarly I wouldn't rush to hold a complete stranger's newborn in the middle of the bank or supermarket as so many people do. Bearing this in mind, imagine what a shock it was to discover that around my 25th birthday I began longing for my own little person. My pregnantness eventually happened when I was 28, but I cried on every birthday in between, only too aware each year that I was another year older and still childless. That was until the winds of change slapped Husband and I hard across the face a few years later.

Husband was already the proud father of his older girls. I became an overnight stepmum to a 6 and 11 year old, nearly ruining everything the first time I was introduced to them by bringing snacks in the form of cookies and PECAN Haagen Daaz. Yes, I tried to kill his children by feeding them nuts. Every sane person that knows anything at all about raising children, which in my defence at the time I didn't, knows you don't allow them to eat nuts until they are at least 21 as they are by far the most evil choking hazard. Husband and our grown up girls still like to remind me about that, and the fact that when the girls had asked what daddy's new girlfriend looked like he had told them I was fat with thick rimmed black glasses. Neither of which were true at the time.

Because Husband already had his brood he wasn't overly interested in producing any more, so when we had a false alarm in the summer before my 28th birthday it was a very serious matter. I decided I would ring Husband from the bus on the way into work to discuss the false alarm, that at that specific time I had no idea was false. This was a trick I'd learnt early on in our relationship and still use now. Never discuss anything face to face the honourable way if there's a chance he might be less than pleased, when I could ring him up and avoid looking him in the eye. Another plus point to this strategy was if the mood was dark on the phone after the admission of whatever I had confessed, he still had the rest of the day before he arrived home to forget/ accept/ get over/ or see the bright side of whatever the given problem was. **You're going to use that now aren't you? You're welcome.**

After explaining that there was a small chance I could be with child if my period, or lack of, were to be believed he was more amiable than I expected. I informed him of my plans to take a test and he instructed me to call him back once I knew one way or the other. Following my lunchtime pregnancy testing activities it was confirmed that it was in fact, a non starter. No one was pregnant, especially not me and I felt like I'd taken a kick in the teeth. No doubt it would be a relief to Husband though. The dial tone rang only twice before Husband answered.

'I've done a test. I've done 3 actually.' I admitted.

SILENCE

'You'll be relieved to know I'm not pregnant.' I spat more peevishly than I'd intended.

SILENCE

'Are you there?' I waited.

'Oh.' He replied in a flat voice.

'I thought you'd be pleased but you don't sound pleased?' I questioned.
   He continued '.... I've been thinking about it this morning and I'd got used to the idea.' **One of many triumphs for my 'phone not face to face' strategy.**

That was the only bit of encouragement I needed. I stopped taking the pill that day and was pregnant for real by the following month.

This time I never gave him the heads up. I'd gone to work as usual and let it slip to the work girls that my period was playing silly buggers again and that there was a chance I might be preggers. Obviously with news as exciting as this I was immediately frog marched to the chemist to buy a test and then made to do it in the staff toilet. Glamorous, no. Necessary, yes. *I think it's important to mention that my highly supportive co workers who are also my very dear friends can be very persuasive about such matters and on suspecting I was pregnant again with my second child a couple of years later, was*

practically held at gunpoint and once again made to do a test in the horribly inappropriate place of the Park n Ride bus station toilet by one of them. Anyway . . .

And there it was. A positive result. In 9 months time I would have a mini me, or a mini him. A sense of relief flowed through me but I was also acutely aware of the huge responsibility that was now mine. A feeling that until then had been alien to me. And it weighed heavily. In an instant I was not only in charge of myself but also for the small life that grew within me, depending solely on me to keep it safe. And this would be my mission. It would have my undivided attention until I met my baby. The mere thought of it blew my mind.

On a Thursday I usually brought home our favourite weekly reads. A magazine for me and a motorcycle newspaper for Husband. On this occasion I'd ditched the usual Marie Claire in favour of something more relevant. Afterall I wouldn't be needing to know '10 ways to wear a tube skirt' or the most up to the minute sex positions. I was going to be a mother soon and would not be fraternizing in the world of tube skirts and certainly wouldnt be 'doing sex'. I was quite sure mothers didn't behave that way. I would adorn long flowing, mother earth type robes, eat organic everything and only give in to sex once a month on date night. Instead I bought myself the latest issue of Mother and Baby magazine and that's how I broke the news to Husband that there would soon be an Anklebiter on the horizon.

In my day dreams about being pregnant I was strong, healthy and glowing. Full of energy like Mother Nature herself but in Human Form. Proudly standing with the swell of my baby bump on show for all to see all of the time, while doing yoga, in a lycra body stocking, listening to whale music. In reality I felt putrid. At least for the first trimester anyway. I had morning sickness that lasted from when I awoke in the morning to the minute I went back to sleep on a night, only interrupted by small pockets of relief when I would sit absolutely still with no movement at all in my head or body, barely breathing to keep movement to a minimum (quite a tricky thing to pull off and not at all practical when there are things to do). There definitely weren't any downward dogs going on or any lycra in sight. The other relief came when I was eating. As I have been a professional eater for the majority of my life this worked out well for me. If I was trenching I felt okay. If ever I'd hoped for a time when it would be acceptable to eat as much as possible for as long as possible to make myself feel good this was it. It also explained the 4 stone I gained during my pregnancy. A particular favourite snack of mine was birthday cake. Let's be clear, I'm not talking about a slice, I'm talking about the whole family size birthday cake. The Skeltons bakery that was situated opposite my work was the shop of choice and I usually went for the vanilla sponge with buttercream and jam filling covered in soft white icing. Delicious. Eaten straight out of the box with a spoon I would go to the edge of the earth to avoid having to share even a small slice with any of the work girls.

As the sickness tapered off, new challenges reared their heads. My day dreams had been right about me loving to flaunt and rub my growing belly beneath floral flowing dresses but had kept quiet about the fatigue, backache and the lack of bowel movements. Not being able to go for a poo even though I felt desperate was fairly traumatic. Wondering if I strained too hard, if I would accidentally push out my baby.

Logically this probably wasn't an actual real threat but all sorts crossed my mind when I was tired, had not toileted a number 2 in over a week and was scared to death of passing a poo the size of my own head. It was around this time that I had to throw in the towel at work. It wasn't viable for me to spend the whole of my work day splitting my time between playing musical statues with myself, eating constantly, taking cat naps and sitting on the crapper for prolonged periods of time worrying if I would birth a poo or a baby right there in the staff toilet.

It always amused me and never got old the way random people in the street would make a beeline straight for my bump, touching and groping it without embarrassment and with no idea who I was. Usually they would be elderly but not always. It seems when you are pregnant, inappropriate fondling without consent is totally fine and publicly accepted. The way people behave around a pregnant person is extremely interesting especially if you are a people watcher as I am, and having a front row seat to witness these oddities was thrilling.

My due date came and went without event. The midwife had called and booked me in for a scratch and sniff, more widely known as a stretch and sweep, to take place the following week. An appointment that sees the midwife put on an enormously long rubber glove up to her armpit and then enter you with it, again up to her armpit. **Well nearly.** From this position, which is uncomfortable for both parties but for different reasons, the midwife will then sweep her hand around the cervix and detach any membrane. This encourages the baby to stop loafing around and get the hell out of there. My appointment was booked for Sunday morning. It all went well. As smoothly as could be expected when a stranger's arm was hanging out from the gaping hole that was once my minge. Straight from the appointment we had to rush off into town to have Husband fitted for a suit for our friend's wedding where he would be an usher. After the procedure I really didn't feel at my best and could feel the baby's head pushing down. Shuffling around after Husband in the suit shop was doing nothing for me. The pressure that I felt between my legs made it feel like the baby might fall out when I was walking. If only. So it was no surprise when the next morning I woke early with a tummy ache.

My hospital bag had been packed for weeks. A huge bag that could have contained my whole life, it actually held tiny baby grows, baby hats and mitts, nappies, toiletries, towels, pjs, breast pads, bum pads and enough pairs of paper pants to sink a battleship. *A little side note about paper pants - they are bloody brilliant and I actually wore them for far longer than was necessary after the birth. After a month or so, Husband had to have a little talk with me to encourage me back into wearing normal underwear. Something I did with great reluctance.* Once I realised it was happening I launched into the action plan I had meticulously mulled over for weeks. I would start with a long relaxing bath, the sort with scented candles and luxurious bubbles. I would wash my hair and check my fanny fuzz situation was still in control thanks to the previous month's wax. *Which just for reference should never ever be done under any circumstances when you are 8 months pregnant, I barely survived.* Once tidy and clean I would dry and style my hair, thoughtfully apply makeup to look cool, possibly even stylish on my entrance to the midwife led birthing centre I had opted for. I would have headphones in to listen to the whale music that would keep me focused while in the throes of labour. Having put this much time and effort into a mammoth amount of careful preparation I would be rewarded with a fast painless mess free birth.

It never happened exactly like that.

By the time I'd managed to lower my bulk into the tepid bubbleless bath, I instantly wanted to get out. It wasn't relaxing or soothing and I was sure I was going to give birth any second, despite being assured previously by the health care professionals that your first baby always takes ages and that you'll have oodles of time. Getting out was more ghastly than getting in because once the baby had engaged into the 'head down' position and my bump had dropped to reflect this I actually had no flexibility at all. Attempting to get out of a bath without being able to bend your body was challenging, infuriating and made me want to cry. On eventually escaping from the bathroom I bounded up the stairs, which was less of a bound and more of a tentative, one step at a time manoeuvre at the speed of a giant tortoise. There was no way any type of makeup or hair styling was happening. My contractions which had started the hour before were becoming more frequent and would not allow me to do anything other than panic. They were super painful and literally stopped me in my tracks, but the pain was more in a severe toothache sort of way than when you've been shot sort of way, or so I imagine. I've never been shot just for the record. At this point my only goal was to get in a pair of paper pants and make it to the hospital before my child came out. Quite a basic goal and definitely a far cry from the previous plan I had fancied.

At this time in our lives Husbands vehicle of choice was a jacked up pick up truck similar to the monster trucks that can be seen on American TV were they drive through lakes and up the sides of buildings. Not really a fitting mode of transport for a pregnant woman that can't lift her leg off the ground more than 3 inches. Once I had been hoisted into the passenger side with the assistance of Husband, we set off. On the 15 minute journey to the birthing centre absolutely everything irritated me. Why was Husband pissing about with the radio? I was seconds away from birthing a small human, probably in the truck because today it didn't seem to be able to go any faster than 30mph which was highly unusual, and he was concerned about which fucking radio station we were listening to? On that journey I felt every tiny lump and bump in the road, every traffic light was at red and all I wanted was for Husband to shut the fuck up. I wanted silence. I wanted calm so I could breathe and zone out. At last I saw the sign for the hospital's birth centre. I'd never seen such a welcoming sight. Finally I was somewhere that knew what was happening and what to do. We pulled up to it and before I knew what was happening went cruising straight by it. 'WHAT'S HAPPENING?! YOU'VE PASSED THE ENTRANCE!!' I shouted angrily in disbelief.

'I'm just going to park up.' Husband informed me. Park up? Was he having a laugh? I could barely walk, probably already had baby limbs poking out of my vagigi and he was going to fucking park up?

'STOP RIGHT NOW. BACK UP AND TAKE ME TO THE DOOR OR I'LL PARK THIS

TRUCK RIGHT UP YOUR ARSE!!' I panted through gritted teeth.

Husband did as he was instructed and let me out at the door to reception and it wasn't a moment too soon. I was taken to a comfortable room with a bed in it. It also had a bathroom which led to a further adjoining room with a birthing pool. The midwife seemed pleasant enough. She showed me around and explained about the birthing pool being available should I want to have a waterbirth. I'd read about water births. They were supposed to ease the pain, be relaxing and be a much less scary introduction to the world for your little person. So long as I didn't have to get my hair wet or need a snorkel I'd definitely consider it.

Husband arrived having successfully parked up and told me he had let my Mum know we were here. My Mum was my other birthing partner. Not overly keen on having Husband present at the birth I'd decided after much deliberation that he had to be there, mainly because I knew he didn't want to be. He found the idea of blood, gore and womens privates being stretched to massive proportions, completely gross. I found this mildly entertaining, so that had been the deciding factor in my decision. He'd also been present both times before at the birth of his older girls and so I didn't see a good enough reason why he should be excused this time.

My contractions were coming thick and fast. It was rather unfortunate however, that every time I had one I did a shit and threw up, all at the same time. Something to do with the baby facing the wrong way and pressing on something that kept making me empty out of both ends. This saw me sitting on the pot with a cardboard bowler hat bedpan for a considerable length of time. Privacy was forbidden so the door remained fully open,enabling the smell to escape along with my dignity. During this time Mum had arrived. Excited at the prospect of her first grandchild which was shortly due to make an appearance, she bustled into the bathroom fussily to greet me on the crapper. The air was green with the smell of unpleasantness but that didn't seem to deter her. 'Hello darling. This is exciting isn't it. I rushed here when I got the call and haven't had a chance to put on my face. **Her makeup, not her actual face.** 'I'll do it now in this mirror. You don't mind, do you? I want to look nice in the photos.'

She was very glamorous, how could I possibly expect her to have a photo taken with her first new born grandchild looking like a horror. 'Help yourself.' I managed, followed by an especially noisy vomit. After mum had finished her makeup I was encouraged by the midwife to have a go in the birthing pool. I couldn't feel any worse so thought I'd give it a whirl. The only thing I felt slightly nervous about was having a floater in the water. Weighing up that I'd been on the toilet for the last hour shitting my head off constantly, I decided that the chances I had anything left to float out were slim to none so I went for it. Stripping naked except for the white vest I was wearing, I waited for my contraction to end and then slowly climbed up the ladder next to the pool and lowered myself in as quickly as I could manage and before the next contraction started. It was a strange feeling. It was like I was in a public swimming pool but semi naked and had spectators inappropriately watching me. I mean, I knew that wasn't what was going on, I hadn't lost the plot completely but that's what it felt like. I'd also resolved months before that I wouldn't have any pain relief. I was drug free so it wasn't that playing tricks on me. Periodically, Husband attempted to touch me. An arm stroke or an encouraging hand on my back but I didn't want to be touched. I wanted everyone to knob off and let me birth my baby alone. It must have been the primal instinct kicking in, that's what I put it down to. A few growls in Husband's direction later, he thought better of the touching and opted for an occasional head pat and a quick retreat instead. Intermittently the midwife would listen to my bump and attach something that monitored the baby's heartbeat. Following the latest check she looked more alert than she had previously and told me I'd have to get out as the heart beat was slow and she needed to have a proper look at me. I sat there waiting for someone to open a secret door that I must have missed until I realised everyone was waiting for me to climb out. Waiting for me to climb back up a 6 foot ladder, naked and with my baby and other gorey bits poking out. A task that if you've never done, it is grossly underestimated. If Husband got a direct view he'd pass out for definite. Eventually after scaling the ladder like I was on the Krypton Factor I managed to crawl to the safety of the next room and took my position on all fours next to the bed as ordered by the midwife. It was at this time approximately 8 people walked in to spectate my child's delivery. Not random passersby but medical students. At least that's what I assumed. Surely random people would much rather go to the theatre or see a film for entertainment on a Monday morning. After finishing her examination it was explained to me that the time had come to push when my next contraction came. Still on all fours on the floor with Husband and Mum holding each of my hands and 8 strangers looking up my rear end I was all set. It was like I was taking a huge poo in a radically public place with spectators, something that really goes against the grain. Programmed from potty training age to poo only on the toilet it was an extremely odd sensation. I knew it's what I had to do yet my body was screaming, 'NOOO, get to the toilet!'

After the first push when the contraction faded and there was no momentum left I was instructed to rest. So I did, and immediately the baby slipped back in. In a breathless sweaty panic I advised the midwife of this.

'Yes that happens I'm afraid.' She told me brightly. She then continued to compare my reproductive system to that of a toilet drainage system, making a direct comparison between the toilet U bend and my birth canal, explaining that once relaxed gravity takes the baby back up the birth canal U Bend pipe (not the toilets). This had to be a sick joke. How long would this go on? Would we still be playing the 'Hokey Cokey' going in and out but not shaking it all about for the next 9 hours? Not on my watch. I was ready. Once the next contraction had subsided and I was told to rest, I did not fucking rest. I continued to push, without the momentum of the contraction. It was hard going, my face was purple, I was lathered in sweat but I wasn't stopping. No progress was made but there was also none of that slipping back in bullshit. A further 2 pushes like this and I was completely spent, but was rewarded with the shrill sound of my newborn baby. I'd done it. And what an empowering feeling. To know that I had expelled a tiny Human from my own body without pain relief and with minimal help, and I hadn't died. I was appalled at the amount of blood though. Obviously I was privy to what happened at a birth but the sheer volume of it shocked me. I apologized for messing up the crisp white bed sheets which I think the room full of onlookers found surprising.

My daughter had arrived. Small and beautiful with a shock of dark hair. She also had a deep tan that would be the envy of all fake bake users, which I later found out was jaundice, apparently common in newborns.

'Who's going to cut the cord?' I heard the midwife enquire in the direction of my birthing partners. Husband visibly paled but before he had the chance to say anything Mum had bagsied the job. 'I'll do it but I need to find my glasses. I want to do a good job, we don't want her to be saddled with an outie for the rest of her life.' Cried mum referring to baby's belly button I presumed. Mum did an excellent job on the cord and also got her first photo, looking every bit as glamorous as she was. Husband had a cuddle with the newest member of his brood and was solely in charge of her while I showered, but shortly after that he explained that he was very tired and needed to have a rest so would be in the comfy chair next to her cot on the ward having a nap. Poor man, I'm sure it must have been exhausting for him to watch me give birth to his daughter. To watch my actual hip bones separate by inches to allow a baby out, to watch my vagigi stretch from the size of a plum to the size of a melon, to watch me physically push another human out of my own body. It makes a lot of sense why women have babies and not men.

One thing I will say is that I was pleasantly surprised by his dedication. He had been due to fly out to Magaluf on a much anticipated stag party the day after, and I made it clear I was happy for him to go, after all I was surrounded by masses of family to help with the little one but he never went.

Husband, we love you.

Our beautiful girl went a whole 3 days with no name. As, much to my devastation the name we had chosen in the event of having a girl never suited her. She just didn't look like what we had picked. On settling on a brand new name selected especially for her we all went home and she was introduced to the wonderful loving crazy family that is ours.

15 Fun Facts about Pregnancy, Birth and the Aftermath

1. While pregnant, complete strangers, usually elderly ladies in public places will lunge out to touch your growing baby bump without permission or explanation.

2. During the later stages of pregnancy your baby will demand you wee during the night as if it were an Olympic sport.

3. The act of pushing out your baby from a hole that is approximately 10 times smaller than the actual baby itself is preferable to the earlier stages of labour

4. When your contraction finishes and you are at rest, the baby slips back in.

5.There is a strong chance that you will have fantasies about having your husband assassinated should he attempt to touch you during labour.

6. Once you have completed 14 hours straight of labour and childbirth without pain relief or intervention your husband will be so exhausted he will need to lay down.

7. Due to pushing out another Human body from your own, your lady holes are now comparable to the Bermuda Triangle in size and mystery.

8. Despite having successfully birthed your 9lb child you will in no way shape or form have a hope in hell of travelling home from the hospital in any other clothing except maternity ones or the duvet cover on your hospital bed.

9. Your first slash following childbirth is worse than the actual childbirth.

10. The probability of having to wee in a warm bath instead of a toilet for the first 3 weeks following the birth is high.

11. In hospital if your milk is slow at making an appearance they hook you up to a cow milking machine.

12. The blue veins in your new feeding boobs resemble an old style road map.

13. If breastfeeding, you will now hold the membership to the 'nipples as long as beer bottles' club.

14. You now own Dolly Parton's actual tits.

15. You become a public flasher. This is because during a breast feed you are not stealthy enough, or have the necessary mount of coordination needed to negotiate your boobs, the breast pads, the muslin square and the easy access maternity bra which is anything but easy access, whilst in Asda, Mamas and Papas, the petrol station, or on a bench in the city centre, all whilst trying not to drop your baby.

The End

Thank you and Big Loves

To my Anklebiters, for not only reading my stories in various stages of completion but for liking them and not being ashamed to laugh out loud at mum's ramblings, even though sometimes the language is a little blue and is totally unsuitable for children. Also for not getting too cross when I've been busy writing and totally ignored you or forgotten to feed you. That's what frozen crumpets are for.

I want to thank Husband, who features frequently throughout my writing, for being a great subject matter and always being comedy gold, most of the time without even knowing. Oh, and let's not forget the sterling piece of advice he gave me about making sure I didn't go on and on at the end of the book, boring everyone to death by thanking everyone from my cousin's boyfriend's sister's cat to a dead pig.

And to my mum who I have bombarded continually with new stuff that I fully expect her to read instantly despite having a fulltime job, a house under renovation and a life.

And to my Dad who wants to read everything I write down because he tells me he is my biggest fan.

And to Auntie who is the only one in the country, probably the world who reads my blog.

Thank you to my friends who have been sounding boards and on occasion, the inspiration for my stories. I apologise that it has been necessary to publicly humiliate you in order to fulfil my dream of writing a book.

To my super clever sister in law Victoria Constable, who inspired me to put pen to paper again after a long time. She wrote and published her very first novel 'Joshua East' a couple of years ago for no other reason than she just felt like it one day. You are a legend.

Finally I give a nod to all those who I have bored the socks off, who have endured years of jackanory time with me. But when all is said and done we all know there's nothing more important in life than a good story.

Coming soon ...

A little Book of Blogs

By Eliza Jong

Release Date Early 2023

Printed in Great Britain
by Amazon